Embedding English and Maths

Practical Strategies for FE and Post-16 Tutors

WITHDRAWN

TERRY SHARROCK

FURTHER
EDUCATION

First published in 2016 by Critical Publishing Ltd

British Library Cataloguing in Publication Data
A CIP record for this book is available from the British Library

ISBN: 978-1-910391-70-9

This book is also available in the following e-book formats:

MOBI ISBN: 978-1-910391-71-6
EPUB ISBN: 978-1-910391-72-3
Adobe e-book ISBN: 978-1-910391-73-0

Cover and text design by Out of House Limited
Project Management by Out of House Publishing
Printed and bound in Great Britain by TJ International Ltd.

Critical Publishing
152 Chester Road
Northwich
CW8 4AL
www.criticalpublishing.com

MIX
Paper from
responsible sources
FSC
www.fsc.org   FSC® C013056

Contents

Meet the author

Terry Sharrock

A qualified teacher, Terry has worked in education for 30 years, both in this country and the United States of America. He has taught literacy and numeracy in schools, colleges and adult and community learning for over 25 years.

Terry was a coach and cohort leader on the National Teaching and Learning Change Programme, designed to improve the teaching of literacy and numeracy in a number of contexts.

He runs his own successful educational consultancy and regularly carries out observations of teaching and learning for a range of providers. Many of the ideas in this book for embedding English and maths skills have been developed from observations of outstanding teaching and learning sessions. He also carries out staff training on embedding maths and English.

Introduction

About this book

This book is written as a result of many years observing learning in a number of contexts, including college classrooms, adult evening classes and work-based learning. It has been written to help tutors to engage and interest learners in the development of their English and maths skills.

It's well documented that young adults in England do not do well in developing their English and maths skills. They regularly appear in the 'relegation zone' of any league tables of English and maths skills.

> "Out of 24 nations, young adults in England (aged 16–24) rank 22nd for literacy and 21st for numeracy. England is behind Estonia, Australia, Poland and Slovakia in both areas."
>
> OECD findings reported in *The Guardian*, 8 October, 2013

While you may argue about the way in which these statistics are arrived at, there is little argument that we need to improve the way English and maths are taught throughout our education system. This book is here to help. Its main aim is to help you as teachers in the further education and skills sector improve the way you develop maths and English skills in your learners. As a teacher in the further education and skills sector, particularly if you are a vocational teacher, you will be under increasing pressure to embed (and this is the word most commonly used) English and maths skills in your lessons. You may have come into teaching to pass on your skills and experience in plumbing or hairdressing but you are now being asked to help develop English and maths skills in learners who quite often have had negative experiences in school and have chosen your subject precisely because they were not successful in the academic subjects of maths and English. This is on top of the numerous other demands on your time, from revised curricula through promoting equality and diversity to achieving outstanding teaching, learning and assessment. And all this with decreasing resources of time and money. The challenge is clear. How can you help learners develop English and maths skills and overcome the negativity they may feel returning to study these subjects? How can you promote an interest in English and maths skills when you may lack confidence in your own skills?

How to use this book

If you are looking for ideas to develop English and maths skills in your teaching, you could go straight to the ideas in the second half of the book and use these directly. However, it will be more effective to take the time to read the first part of the book and think about your current teaching and how successful you are in helping learners to really understand, develop and apply their English and maths skills.

Most tutors are hardworking, committed teachers striving to do the best for their learners in very challenging circumstances. If you have bought this book you are probably one of those. Tutors are asked to develop English and maths skills and are often not given clear guidance on how to do this most effectively. People do not try to do a bad job, but they are often confused about what their role is in helping to embed and develop English and maths skills. In addition they may lack ideas about how they can do it most effectively. The ideas in this book come from many years of observing lessons and from developing well-regarded training sessions for tutors. Lessons can inspire and motivate learners or they can stultify and frustrate learners. The ideas presented in this book work. It is common for lesson plans to state that they will embed and develop English and maths skills, but this is often not translated into action. Some lesson planning only serves to pay lip service or complete a 'tick box' to satisfy the perceived need of some external body such as an inspection agency or observer from a management team. This tick-box exercise is of little benefit to anybody.

This book talks about what is really meant by embedding English and maths skills and how it relates to development of skills. It also suggests some ideas you may use in your teaching and learning in tried and tested ways that will engage and motivate your learners.

The structure of this book

Part 1

Chapter 1 What does embedding English and maths skills really mean?

The first chapter in the book discusses the meaning of 'embedding' and how it relates to skills development. It considers what makes outstanding embedding of English and maths skills and gives examples of learners' writing to highlight the issue of addressing lack of achievement at school. It discusses issues of marking written work and looks at the most effective ways of giving feedback to learners and setting targets that lead to real develop-ment of English and maths skills. There is a discussion of how to record the progress of learners in the development of skills, so that improvements are clear to see. It suggests how best to assess written work so that learners are motivated to improve. There is a discussion of how to deal with different forms of learners' writing, including the use of 'text speak'. It concludes with a look at why developing English and maths skills is so important.

Chapter 2 What are the barriers to learning and how can they be overcome?

This chapter discusses why many learners are reluctant to engage in learning English and maths. It explores some of the most common barriers to learning, such as lack of confidence and a negative history of English and maths skills development in previous education.

It draws on research into learners' attitudes towards English and maths and relates these findings to learner behaviour, engagement and motivation. There is a discussion based on recent research which highlights negative attitudes among learners, particularly towards maths, and suggests practical strategies to overcome these, including how to show learners that everybody can 'do' maths. It discusses organisational approaches to developing English and maths skills and considers the merits of different methods, giving examples of the most effective methods of embedding and developing English and maths across the organisation. This chapter also considers research findings looking at the kinds of English and maths skills employers are looking for and relating this to the English and maths skills that learners need to develop.

Finally the chapter looks at the requirements of the revised Common Inspection Framework (September 2015) and its implications for post-16 providers. There is discussion of what Ofsted inspectors and post-16 quality managers are looking for when making judgements on the effectiveness of embedding and developing English and maths skills and what makes for outstanding provision.

Chapter 3 How we learn and remember

This chapter looks at one particularly effective approach to the question of how learners understand and remember concepts in English and maths, such as mathematical terms and spellings. It gives examples of using this method to remember people's names and extends this to ways to remember key concepts in maths as well as using it as one method to remember spellings. It discusses the concepts of a 'learning' classroom and a 'teaching' classroom and examines the difference, to explain, for example, why learners often have difficulties in recalling content that has been taught. It outlines a strategy for learning which encourages learners to make connections in order to understand, remember and apply key concepts. It gives examples of the use of learning logs to monitor progress and concludes with a discussion of other methods to improve spellings.

Chapter 4 Case studies in embedding English and maths

This chapter focuses on four case studies of teaching sessions that were judged and agreed by both an internal manager and an external practising inspector. The case studies cover the range of learning, with judgements from 'Inadequate', 'Requires Improvement' and 'Good', through to 'Outstanding'. Each case study includes a commentary on the session and an opportunity to reflect on what makes it effective and how it could be improved.

PART 2

Practical activities

The second part of the book is a collection of 20 practical activities for you to use to embed and develop English and maths skills in your lessons. There are ten activities to help embed maths skills, followed by ten activities focused on English skills. The left-hand page provides a set of guidance notes for you, the tutor. The notes include: suggestions on how and why you might use the idea; an explanation of how to carry out the activity; the key skills that might be developed and practised; specific employability skills that are developed; and possible extension activities. The right-hand pages feature the activity itself, describing it and, where necessary, providing clear instructions for the learner.

Free resources

All the student activities may be photocopied free of charge and they are also available as free downloads from the publisher's website: www.criticalpublishing.com.

Reference

Ramesh, R (2013) 'England's young people near bottom of global league table for basic skills', *The Guardian*, 8 October. Available at: www.theguardian.com/education/2013/oct/08/england-young-people-league-table-basic-skills-oecd (accessed 21 July 2015).

PART 1
The importance of
embedding English and maths
in your lessons

Chapter 1 What does embedding English and maths skills really mean?

"The best way to predict the future is to create it."

Abraham Lincoln

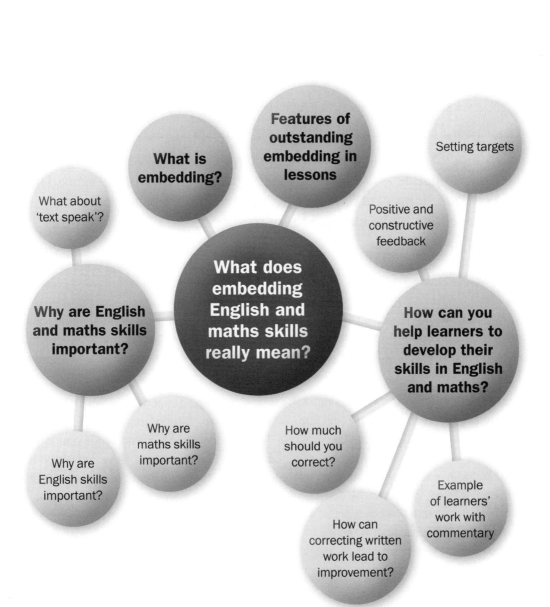

Introduction

This chapter considers what outstanding embedding of English and maths looks like; the purpose of embedding; how best to feed back on learners' written work; and how to help learners understand the importance of developing English and maths skills.

Tutors in further education are constantly being asked to 'embed' English and maths into their teaching. A lot of time and effort is spent on this and observers are keen to see 'embedding' in practice. However, less time is spent on coming to a common understanding of what 'embedding' is and why it might be desirable in the development of English and maths skills in learners.

What is embedding?

In 2003 the Skills for Life Strategy Unit defined embedding as follows:

> " *Embedded teaching and learning combines the development of literacy, language and numeracy with vocational and other skills. The skills acquired provide learners with the confidence, competence and motivation necessary for them to succeed in qualifications, in life and in work.* "
>
> **Skills for Life Strategy Unit, DfES, 2003**

Embedding, as the definition says, is the development of literacy, language and numeracy (more commonly referred to now as English and maths skills) alongside the development of vocational and other skills so that learners can increase in 'confidence, competence and motivation'.

Notice the use of the word 'developing'. Ask yourself, why is it so important to embed English and maths into lessons? What is the purpose of embedding? Put simply, it is to help learners develop these skills, so that they can use them confidently to succeed in qualifications, in life and in work. The only purpose of embedding is to help develop skills. Think about that, and whenever you hear the word 'embedding', link it with the development of skills. If embedding is not leading to the development of English and maths skills then it is a waste of time: it becomes a tick-box exercise and another piece of paperwork which has no impact on learners. Think less about meeting the needs of observers, management and inspection agencies and focus more on how you can best develop the English and maths skills that learners need and that so many of them lack.

Features of outstanding embedding in lessons

Consider the following activity. It might be something you would want to do as part of staff development or as a discussion point in a staff meeting.

Reflective Task

Imagine you are sitting in a lesson, or watching a one-to-one session in a work-based learning context. It strikes you that the embedding of English and maths in this lesson is outstanding.

What makes you come to this judgement?

Ask yourself what is happening in the lesson?

What are the learners doing?

What is the tutor doing?

In other words, consider what outstanding embedding of English and maths looks like in practice.

What would the learning environment look like?

What behaviours are displayed and what interactions are happening between tutor and learners or between learner and learner?

Take a few moments to think about this or discuss it with someone else before you move on.

A number of things would be happening. Some characteristics of an outstanding lesson are listed in the table.

Characteristics	Notes
There is an atmosphere of mutual respect in the lesson.	Learners are interested in their learning. Interested learners are enthusiastic and they feel confident to discuss their work, both with the tutor and with each other.
Learners are encouraged to contribute to discussion in the lesson.	The time spent talking in the lesson is split at least 50:50 between tutor and learners. In too many lessons the time split is often 80:20 in favour of the tutor and sometimes learners don't even contribute 20 per cent of the time. If learners are sitting passively for most of the time then it is likely that they are not being given the chance to make the most of their learning opportunity.

Characteristics	Notes
Learners are confident in talking about their learning.	In the best lessons you can see and hear the learning taking place. Learners are confident to talk about their learning. They are happy and comfortable to discuss their uncertainties and misconceptions. They are given plenty of opportunities to work in pairs or small groups and learn from each other.
Learners are encouraged to explore and learn from their mistakes.	Learners are not afraid to make mistakes. In fact mistakes can be encouraged and celebrated. Certainly the working atmosphere in the lesson would be one where learners feel safe to express their uncertainty without fear of ridicule. They would feel secure in the knowledge that concepts in maths and English that they find confusing will be explored and explained until they become confident in their meaning and their applications.
There is a good learning environment.	The room itself would be conducive to good learning, with stimulating material which is referred to and made use of. You might expect to see displays showing explanations of common concepts in English and maths. More importantly, these displays would be made use of in the lesson.
The lesson is well planned.	There is clear evidence that the tutor has given some thought to the planning of the lesson to identify areas where embedding and development of English and maths skills might occur and what opportunities there might be to develop these skills. The tutor would have looked at the scheme of work and lesson planning and identified areas where the development of English and maths skills could occur as a natural part of the content.
Learners are aware of the importance of developing English and maths skills.	There is a clear feeling that learners understand the importance and the relevance of improving English and maths skills. They have bought into the idea of improving their skills. For example, when carrying out any activities the tutor clearly explains how the activity helps to develop English and maths skills and ensures that the learners understand how what they are being asked to do will result in improving skills.

Example

In one college I visited, I was very impressed with some large colourful posters that lined the wall leading to the college cafeteria. The posters explained concepts such as homonyms and gave eye-catching examples involving cute pictures of puppies with the caption 'Is that your dog?' and pictures of baby twins exclaiming 'You're so like me'. In this way the different uses of 'your' and 'you're' were explained in an interesting and engaging way. However, when I asked the tutors what use they made of these interesting and engaging posters, they were unable to give an example. Wasn't it enough that they were up there? It's as if they expected learners to develop skills by osmosis, by simply walking past these posters! There is something to suggest that their presence might be useful, but how much more useful if the tutor could point them out and then, perhaps, ask them to spend a few seconds looking at the poster next time they were going to the cafeteria and perhaps think of examples for themselves or at a convenient time give a short presentation to the class on the different uses of the words.

How can you help learners to develop their skills in English and maths?

Let's start by having a look at an example of a piece of work from a learner. This may or may not be typical of the standard of work that you see on a daily basis from your learners. Your learners may be more or less skilful in their use of English than the actual example given below. However, the principle remains the same: you need to think about how you should respond to written work from learners in ways that encourage them to improve their use of English.

Example

The scene is a general further education college, seven weeks into a first-year IT course. Students are developing skills in computer animation and games design. The author is a young student starting out on her college course. This is what she wrote.

"I'm oly gust from Secondery school so all this is new to me. I like animals and sciance. I love art. I would love to be an animater when I am older (the Dremworks). I'lld love to run it. (to become a produser of my one cumpany) and I really hope to finsh this corse and inprove my Ingalish and my horid speillings"

And this is what she meant.

"I'm only just from secondary school, so all this is new to me. I like animals and science. I love Art. I would love to be an animator when I am older (the DreamWorks). I'd love to run it (to become a producer of my own company) and I really hope to finish this course and improve my English and my horrid spellings."

Commentary on example

There are a few things to say about this piece. One of the first is that this learner has gone through at least 11 years of schooling. Eleven years of working on and practising her written English. It seems almost unbelievable that she could still be writing in this way after that, but this is the case. And she is not alone, or by any means the least skilful writer that you may come across. As educators in the post-16 learning and skills sector, what are we meant to do with such learners? The simple answer is 'our best'. Many tutors say, 'If they didn't get these things right in 11 years of schooling, how are we meant to turn it around in a year or less?' They have a point. It seems an impossible task to move this learner from what you see above, to a confident and accurate writer of English. But consider the alternative. If we do nothing and concentrate solely on developing her skills as a games designer, how will she fare? It is unlikely that she would be employed in any capacity with such a poor standard of written English, and that is to disregard the effect of this level of literacy on her everyday life. So 'doing nothing' is not an option. Most educators in the post-16 sector want to do something, they just lack the confidence or guidance to know what to do.

Positive and constructive feedback

Written feedback on work, done correctly, can have a powerful effect on learners' views of themselves as writers and lead to real improvements in confidence. There are a number of key factors which make for positive and constructive feedback.

» The first thing to do is to acknowledge this piece of writing. Pay attention to it. The piece of writing above was done in the first weeks of the course, and seven weeks into the course the tutor had still not read it. This is a great shame and it sends a message that if it can be ignored in this way, writing is not important.

» In your feedback look for the good in any piece of writing. Sometimes tutors are too keen to say what is wrong with a piece of writing, when they could look for what is right about it. This piece is very heartfelt. If it was spelt and punctuated correctly it would be a very good example of a personal piece of writing. First of all, the learner should be praised for being so honest and expressing herself so well. However, you cannot ignore that there are conventions of written English that this piece does not follow.

» Ensure that writing is something that you, as a tutor, are interested in. Encourage learners to share their writing and compare it with their peers'.

Practical Task

Next time you ask learners to do any writing, have a go at the same exercise yourself. Show them that what you are doing is valuable enough for you to do it yourself as well. You might even want to share what you have done and compare it to your learners' efforts.

Setting targets

Get into the habit of setting learners targets to improve English and maths just as you might set them targets to improve their vocational skills. Share these targets with learners. Involve them in the process of setting them and celebrate the achievement of these targets, however small. With the learner above, you might acknowledge that it is an interesting piece and she has expressed herself very well. However, as she says, the spelling might be described as 'horrid' and you are going to work with her to improve that. Talk about how you will be working together over the course of the programme to develop her skills as a games creator and a very important part of that is to develop skills in English and maths.

How much should you correct?

Perhaps you feel that as a tutor you should highlight every error of spelling and punctuation. This is one approach but one that needs to be handled with care so as not to discourage learners from engaging in writing in the future. One of the negative effects of highlighting every error is that learners can get disheartened and often adopt the tactic of not writing very much, on the basis that the less they write, the less there is to get wrong. Start with the positive. You might wish to adopt a system of self- and/or peer-assessment of written work. You could produce a simple pro forma, either electronic or paper-based so learners can get into the habit of self- or peer-assessing their own work. You can use this as a matter of course, encouraging learners to complete it before handing in written work. Examples of self-assessment sheets (one for English and one for maths) are given in Appendices 3 and 4. These are only examples. You can, of course, adapt them or devise similar assessment sheets of your own. If you establish this habit of self- and peer-assessment and make it part of your everyday teaching, it can have a significant effect on the improvement of learners' maths and English skills, as well as handing some ownership for identifying errors in maths and English over to the learner.

How can correcting written work lead to improvement?

In looking at hundreds of pieces of marked work over the years, one thing that strikes me is how little improvement results from tutors' feedback on written work. Post-16 educators spend a lot of time going through work and correcting it but often without an effective system to ensure that these corrections are adopted and lead to improvements in written work. Typically comments are 'Watch your spelling', 'Be careful with capital letters', or words that are spelt incorrectly are circled or underlined, possibly with 'sp' in the margin. Tutors spend a lot of time and effort on this, but does it lead to improvements? Ask learners what they are expected to do with this feedback and you might be surprised to find that you are met with blank looks. It is important to put time and effort into establishing a system for what learners do with feedback on written work. For example, you might want them to establish their own paper or electronic spelling logs. These can be referred to when writing. Chapter 3 looks at what works in improving skills such as spelling and Appendix 2 contains an example of a spelling log that you may wish to adopt. For now, try this simple strategy.

Practical Task

Next time you write 'sp' in the margin or underline an incorrect spelling of a word add the number '3' to it, so you might write 'sp3'. Help learners out by underlining only the part of the word which is incorrectly spelt. Learners rarely spell whole words incorrectly. Look at the example from the computer animation student above. Even here, only parts of words are misspelt. Get learners into the habit of knowing that when they see 'sp3' next to a word, it means that you would like them to find and write out – or add to their spelling logs – three words that end in the same pattern. For example, the learner above has written 'improve' as 'inprove'. Using 'sp3' you might encourage her to find the correct spellings of three words with a similar spelling pattern. At first you could provide vocationally relevant words as she is on a computer games design course, eg, 'import'. You might expand this to more general words such as 'important' or 'impress'. As her confidence grows she may be able to find words herself when she sees the 'sp3' on her work. The point is that there is a system which is understood by the learners that records improvements in spellings.

This is one example of an approach to improving and recording improvements in English and maths skills. The spelling log becomes a record of progress that learners can be proud of. You can use written work to show progress over time, and, more importantly, as a motivation for learners to show them how they are improving. An additional bonus is that this provides evidence for external observers of how learners are improving.

Why are English and maths skills important?

Outstanding embedding and development of English and maths skills is founded on one simple underlying idea. English and maths are important. Developing these skills is worthwhile and essential, but it doesn't have to be tedious. Activities can be fun!

Why are English skills important?

One of the questions that learners often ask is why is it important to spell and punctuate correctly or why, for example, if they are on an art course, they need to add up or multiply correctly? The most common complaint of learners is 'Why does it matter?' 'My friends understand what I am saying and even if I spell things wrong or don't use the right punctuation, you can still understand what I'm saying, can't you?' It's a well-rehearsed argument and one that has some validity. Only in the most extreme cases (and the example above is getting near that) is understanding what is written an issue. Take a look at the piece below, which variously claims to be research by Oxford or Cambridge scientists. While this is most likely to be false, the point is still valid. Have a go yourself and see what you think.

Practical Task

Look at the piece of writing below. After looking at it for a few moments, you should be able to understand what it says, although only the first and last letters of each word are correct.

"rscheearchs at Ofoxrd Uinervtisy hvae mdae an itneinerstg driecsovy. If you tkae any pecie of wntriig and keep olny the frist and lsat ltteer of ervey wrod in the crocret pacle, but jmulbe up the rset of the ltetres, the wntriig wlil slitl mkae snsee. Tihs is bcuseae the huamn brain olny nedes the fsirt and lsat lteter as a cule and it can flil in the rset."

Can you understand it? If so, it makes the point that incorrect spelling is not necessarily a major obstacle to understanding. If we can be understood with random spelling, then, as our learners sometimes say, 'Why bother?' We bother because spelling and punctuation is about more than understanding – it's about making an impression. Every time they commit words to paper, or more commonly these days text to their electronic devices, learners are creating an impression. You have never met the learner whose writing was quoted earlier (who one day hopes to be the director of a computer animation company), but you have formed an impression of her from her writing. You are making all sorts of assumptions about her education, her social status and her intelligence. Would you give her a job or trust her to communicate in writing to customers? Probably not. Learners need to understand that writing makes an impression and decide what kind of impression they want to create in the future. It's your job to help them make the best impression they can.

Creating a good impression and developing skills of reading, writing, speaking and listening can have a positive effect across all subjects. Increasing confidence in any of these aspects of English can help learners develop skills in all their subjects. They are better able to read and understand and are more confident in contributing to discussions. This is vital in preparing them for their future. All their future work and study will involve demonstrating these skills – from writing job applications to creating presentations to reading and understanding written information. Talking to customers in the hospitality industry, writing reports for managers and customers and presenting text for websites, blogs and marketing materials are just a few of the many skills that learners will need for their future.

What about 'text speak'?

One of the most common complaints of tutors and employers is the use of 'text speak' instead of properly constructed sentences. There are all kinds of written communication and learners need help to understand that in different contexts we all communicate, both in writing and orally, in different ways. We are expert at moving between these different types of spoken and written English. We take it for granted that we adjust the way we write as we move between informal notes, texts and emails to close friends, relatives and work colleagues and more formal language we might use in more 'public' documents. It's the same with speech. We move effortlessly through different ways of speaking according to the situation that we are in. We talk in a different way according to our situation. We use different vocabulary, tones and even dialect and accent according to our audience. We wouldn't address an interview panel in the same way that we might talk to our friends in a social setting. Learners need help to understand that none of these ways of speaking (or writing) is less important than another, but that they need to be aware of their audience and adjust their method or style of communication accordingly. Confusion arises when people adopt a way of speaking or writing which is not suited to the audience. Some people might have difficulty understanding some of the text speech that learners are so adept at, but for them in their social circles it is perfectly acceptable (and you might argue culturally necessary) to communicate in this way. You can help them develop this versatility to move between different modes of speech and writing by helping them with their English skills. This is not an easy job and it is made more difficult by the barriers to developing English and maths skills that many learners bring with them.

Why are maths skills important?

Maths skills are important, but learners need persuading of this. They need to see that they can develop maths skills and use them in a number of situations. It's essential in life and work to be able to deal with numbers and be confident to engage with and solve problems that involve numbers. It's this lack of confidence that holds back so many learners. From budgeting money to telling the time; from understanding percentages to estimating how long it will take you to travel somewhere; from probability of rainfall through mobile phone contracts to calculating discounts on sales items, students encounter maths every day. Most jobs require aspects of maths. A few examples include: hairdressers, who may use percentage and ratios to mix colours; construction workers estimating and measuring distance as well as using formulas to convert units of measurement. Learners involved in animal welfare may need to monitor changes in weight as well as calculate the cost of keeping an animal. Maths is needed in almost every job from computing to engineering and catering to business administration and customer service. In all cases learners need to understand the importance of maths and to have the belief that they can engage confidently with numbers.

In convincing learners that maths is important, it is essential to take a wider view of what maths is. Many learners associate maths with meaningless numbers and unintelligible formulas, often related to their experience at school. The study of maths gives learners the opportunity to develop skills that are vital for their future success. Maths helps develop skills such as team working, problem solving and – in a world where we are overloaded with data – the skills of reading and interpreting information. It also provides opportunities to practise skills in filtering out information. Most of the real-life and vocational maths problems that learners will encounter in their lives will either contain too much or too little information to solve the problem that is presented. Learners will have to make decisions on what information is important and what can be discarded. They need to develop the skills to find information which is not provided, but is often essential to finding the solution. The study of maths-related problems also gives learners the opportunity to practise and develop skills of perseverance and problem solving, rather than giving up at the first sign of difficulty. Tutors should consider how to bring this wider view of maths to their learners and how to overcome the resistance that learners have, particularly but not exclusively, to learning maths.

Next steps

The next chapter looks at the barriers that learners bring to the development of English and maths skills, where these barriers come from and what you can do to overcome them.

Chapter 2 What are the barriers to learning and how can they be overcome?

"Whether you think you can, or you think you can't – you're right."

Henry Ford

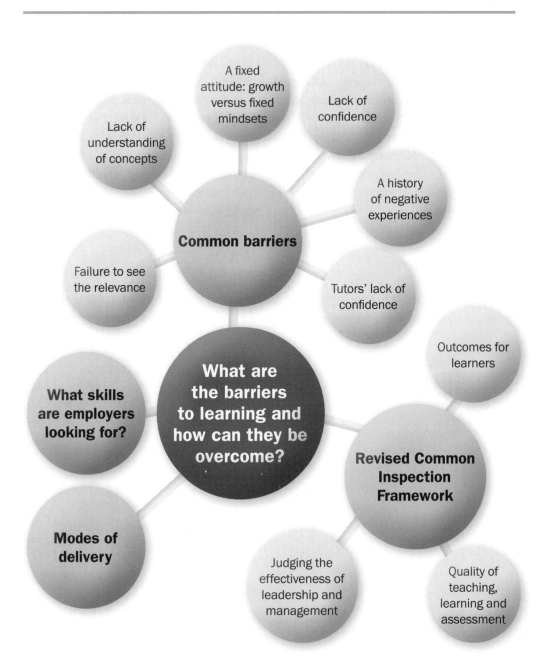

Introduction

This chapter looks at the most common barriers that learners face in developing English and maths skills. It discusses attitudes towards English and maths and how to overcome the attitude of students who feel that they are not able to make progress. It examines research into fixed and growth mindsets with reference to maths skills. It also looks at how anxiety, particularly in maths, can affect students' attitudes towards developing skills. It discusses the role of the tutor and looks at delivery models, highlighting the advantages and disadvantages of each. It examines research into what English and maths skills employers are looking for. Finally, it discusses how the development of English and maths skills will be judged and what criteria the revised Ofsted Common Inspection Framework will use to assess providers' quality of delivery.

Common barriers

Let's start with the most common barriers to developing English and maths skills. In my experience of observing teaching and learning sessions, and from discussions with practitioners, these are:

» a fixed attitude towards developing English and maths skills;

» a lack of confidence;

» a history of negative experience;

» failure to see the relevance of developing English and maths skills;

» a lack of understanding of concepts;

» deliverers' lack of confidence.

A fixed attitude: growth versus fixed mindsets

Perhaps the most significant barrier to improving maths and English is the learners' attitude to developing these skills. In her book *Mindset: The New Psychology of Success* (Dweck, 2006), Harvard professor Carol Dweck identified two types of attitude towards maths in learners. Some learners have a 'growth mindset' and others have a 'fixed mindset'. Essentially learners with a fixed mindset believe that maths ability is a gift and no amount of practice will lead to improvement in these skills. Learners with a 'growth mindset', on the other hand, believe that maths skills can be developed and improved with practice. Specifically, the research found that learners with a growth mindset:

» believe that maths ability can be developed and improved over time;

» view mistakes as an opportunity to develop;

» are resilient;

» believe that effort creates success;

» think about how they learn.

Whereas learners with a fixed mindset:

» believe that being 'good' at maths is something you are born with and can't change;

» are reluctant to take on challenges;

» prefer to stay in their comfort zone;

» are fearful of making mistakes;

» think it is important to 'look smart' in front of others.

Adapted from Hindle, n.d.

This research looked specifically at maths learners, but many of the findings would apply equally to learners who have problems with English.

Many learners in further education have adopted a fixed mindset in developing their maths and English skills. This shows itself most commonly through fixed ideas and comments such as 'I was never any good at maths (or spelling)' and 'You're either good at maths/English or you're not. And I'm not!' These attitudes are in evidence every day and the challenge for you is to encourage learners to let go of the fixed mindset and replace it with a 'growth' mindset. So, how can you encourage students to have a growth mindset?

» Constantly remind students that ability in English and maths is not fixed and can be improved with effort and persistence. Log progress of students to show them how they have improved.

» Provide formative feedback that gives credit for the strategies used and the approach, even if the final answer in maths is incorrect or the final draft or presentation could be improved.

» Recognise effort and reward the resilience of students who keep going with problems, particularly when they encounter difficulties. Praise students for their efforts at least as much as for finding the correct answer.

» Encourage students to reflect on mistakes and see these as a positive part of the learning process. Get them to think about how they approached the problem and identify the difficulties and try to learn from these. A useful acronym for your learning environment is:

MISTAKES = Means I Start To Acquire Knowledge, Experience (and) Skills.

» Help students understand that people learn at different speeds and this is acceptable. Students will naturally compete against each other but as a tutor it is your job to ensure that students are encouraged to make progress as an individual rather than constantly comparing themselves, negatively, against others.

Lack of confidence

Many students (and tutors) display a lack of confidence. Many students have not had success at school or may have experienced failure in exams. Maths anxiety (and, to a lesser extent, English anxiety) is a recognised problem, and research has shown that maths anxiety can prevent engagement with number problems

Dr Vinod Menon and a team at Stanford University in the USA carried out research into maths anxiety. A number of students were chosen, some with high maths anxiety and some with low anxiety. Brain scans were carried out on students as they worked on maths problems. Students with high anxiety responded to maths problems in the same way others might respond to phobias such as snakes and spiders. As their anxiety levels increased, so the part of the brain that deals with problem solving closed down and students were more inclined to give up on the problem (Digitale, 2012). It's this disengagement at the outset that makes development of maths skills so difficult. You need to rebuild your learners' confidence in English and maths. The first step, in maths particularly, is to start to dispel the myth that some people just can't do it. Try the example below to help them consider this.

Example

When learners say they can't do maths ask them to consider how many times in their lives they have crossed the road on their own. They may seem a little confused about the connection but ask them to bear with you. Ask them to think about what they do every time they cross the road. They stop at the kerb and if a car is approaching, they estimate the distance of the car, they estimate the speed of the car, they estimate the distance to the other side of the road and they estimate how fast they can walk. They put all this information into the decision-making part of the brain and in a fraction of a second they carry out an amazingly complex calculation and come up with an answer whether to cross or not. If another car is approaching at the same time, the complexity of the calculation is even greater, but it does not deter the brain from building that into the calculation and making a decision. You might conclude by, light-heartedly, reminding them that if they got the answer wrong they probably wouldn't be in the class!

Realising that everybody is capable of some amazing maths calculations can be the start of rebuilding learners' confidence with maths. As a tutor you have to remind learners regularly that everybody can 'do maths'.

A history of negative experiences

Linked to their lack of confidence, you may find that many of your learners have a history of negative experiences with maths and English. Try this activity, perhaps as part of your continuous professional development or at a team meeting.

Practical Task

Work in pairs. The first person should describe their best-ever learning experience. It could be any learning. It does not have to be confined to formal education. It could be learning to ride a bike or learning to swim.

Allow five minutes to talk about that experience to your partner. Your partner should listen and ask questions to find out more about the experience, and try to pick out the key features of what made it such a good experience, noting these down in words or short phrases.

Swap over. Your partner now has five minutes to explain their best learning experience, while you listen, ask questions and note down the key words or phrases used to explain what made it such a good experience.

Compare notes and create a joint list of the key components of a really good learning experience. (See Appendix 1 for some of the key components that regularly feature in this activity.)

Finally, take five minutes each to talk about your worst learning experience. Pick out the key components of your worst learning experience and compare them with your best.

In general, the key points that arise from bad learning experiences are:

» not understanding what was being explained;

» not seeing the relevance of what they are learning to practical applications;

» poor teaching in terms of impatient teachers who do not explain or cannot understand why the learner doesn't 'get it';

» experience of sarcasm and demeaning comments about their abilities (and even public humiliation), leading to feelings of inadequacy.

Such experiences can have a lasting and profound effect on learners' self-image. These (often disengaged) learners need help to develop a new self-image where they can be successful. Some of the ways you can do this are as follows.

» Always explain what skills you are aiming to develop when you give students a task. Explain why they are doing something; what skills it will develop and how it might relate to real life. For example, in a problem involving percentages, explore what a percentage is and why you would need to know about percentages. Examples might include: money off sales items; interest rates on loans or credit cards; and responses to surveys such as '23 per cent of people disagreed'.

» Allow learners plenty of time to work together and discuss the learning. Encourage them to explain concepts such as decimals or the use of apostrophes to each other so that they can frame their understanding in their terms.

» Make learning interactive and look for the fun element in any learning. Use short, focused fun activities to highlight the use of English and maths.

» Be patient. If a learner doesn't understand one method, change the method. Learners' reasons for negativity are many and varied and we have to adopt many and varied strategies to rebuild confidence.

» Think about what you say to learners. Reflect on the kind of comments that you make. Could any of these be seen as derogatory or sarcastic? Think carefully about what you say. Apparently offhand comments can have a profound effect on learners' confidence.

Failure to see the relevance

One of the key factors in a lack of success with English and maths is a failure to see the relevance of these subjects to their lives. Most students are generally unquestioning and will carry out exercises that tutors give them (with varying degrees of enthusiasm!). Students engage in English and maths activities without ever really exploring why they are doing them or how engaging in the activity can help develop valuable life skills. Consider how you introduce activities. When you explain the task, how much time do you allocate to explaining why they should do it and, particularly, what skills are being developed in this task? Be specific.

Practical Task

You decide to use a word-search activity. It usually takes the form of a box of random letters with words hidden among them. Ask yourself, what skills are you trying to develop in your students? How is completing a word-search box helping develop English or maths skills? The hidden words may be vocational terms that students need to be familiar with, or perhaps mathematical terms. Are you trying to develop an understanding of these terms and how students may use them? Are you trying to improve the spelling of these words? You may be doing both of these or something else. Whatever you are trying to do, ask yourself, 'Have I made this sufficiently clear so that my students understand what skills they are developing and why?'

You need to help students to see the relevance of developing English and maths skills in terms of both qualifications and skills that they will need and use through their lives. You can do this by adopting the habit of explaining the relevance and importance of each activity.

Lack of understanding of concepts

Many students experience difficulties with English and maths because they do not fully understand some basic concepts. Failure to understand basic concepts can be compared to trying to build a house without secure foundations. For example there is no point in trying to develop a construction worker's skill in mixing ratios of sand and cement if they have no idea what a ratio is.

Take time to explain concepts. Ensure that students understand and can apply concepts. How many times do you ask a whole group a question and then accept the answer of one student and move on without really checking whether the whole group has understood? When one person answers, you may know that person has grasped the concept, but what about the others? This is one of the drawbacks of whole-class question and answer. The majority of students can be left behind without an opportunity to express their lack of understanding. It takes a brave and confident student to say that they don't understand.

Example

When carrying out whole-class discussion or revision activities, if you say 'Do you all understand that?' and there is no answer, don't accept that and move on. Find some way to check the understanding of each individual in the group. You could ask individuals to answer. You could divide the group into pairs and ask one to explain the concept to another. When this is done ask the one who has had it explained to explain to the rest of the group. The use of individual whiteboards can greatly enhance the checking of students' understanding. When students are in the habit of using interactive whiteboards to answer questions it becomes much easier to see which students have understood and can apply concepts, discuss common misconceptions and clarify them.

Tutors' lack of confidence

Your attitude as a tutor is crucial to the successful development of English and maths skills. Tutors' anxieties or uncertainties are easily transferred to students, often unconsciously. If tutors lack confidence or competence in developing English and maths skills they will avoid these in case their own shortcomings are exposed. This is understandable. It is crucial for post-16 providers to have a clear policy on the role of the tutor in the development of skills. Tutors must understand what part they play in the development of these skills in their students. If they are being asked to be solely responsible for improving English and maths skills then they must also have access to the necessary professional development to help them prepare for this role. Only when they are absolutely clear about their role can they be confident about how to carry out that role. This clarity of role arises from a clearly explained and understood mode of delivery.

Modes of delivery

Table 2.1 below shows three of the most common modes of delivery, together with the advantages and disadvantages of each.

Table 2.1 Modes of delivery

Mode	Explanation	Advantages	Disadvantages
Separate delivery	This is where the delivery of the vocational content and the development of English and maths are completely separate. Students attend separate classes to develop English and maths skills.	Specialist tutors provide subject expertise on English and maths.	Students see English and maths and their vocational area as two separate subjects. This reduces the effect of integration and embedding of skills so that students fail to see the relevance of English and maths in their vocational area.
Totally integrated	This is where the development of English and maths skills is solely the responsibility of the vocational tutor.	Students see the relevance of English and maths in the vocational area and benefit from integration of English and maths in a vocational context.	Some vocational staff may lack confidence and competence in teaching certain areas, particularly higher-level English and maths skills.
Mixed delivery	Vocational tutors and English and maths subject specialists work together to develop students' English and maths skills.	English and maths skills are integrated into the vocational area. Students see the relevance of these skills. Students benefit from a combination of vocational and specialist tutor input, particularly in the higher levels of English and maths skills.	Requires good systems of communication and close communication between the specialist and vocational tutors.

Although totally integrated and separate delivery models have their advantages, the most effective delivery model is the mixed one, where vocational tutors and specialist English and maths tutors work closely together to support students to see the relevance and importance of developing these skills.

What skills are employers looking for?

In overcoming barriers to developing English and maths skills, one area that students need to be aware of is the kind of skills employers are looking for. Surveys carried out over many years reveal that employers are concerned about the lack of English and maths skills of people entering the world of work. It seems as if this is a perennial problem. Employers say that people coming to them lack fundamental skills in English and maths and yet students often complain about, and fail to see the importance of, developing these skills. You are caught in the middle!

Making Maths and English Work for All is a survey by the Education and Training Foundation (Pye Tait Consulting, 2015). Research was carried out over a period of four and a half weeks, involving 600 employers and almost 500 educational practitioners. Data was gathered from a wide variety of sources including online surveys, telephone surveys, face-to-face discussions and through workshops with employers, practitioners and learners. The research found that:

» 75 per cent of employers feel that action is required at a national level to improve English and maths;

» employers are less satisfied with the level of ability in English compared to maths;

» 46 per cent of employers are most concerned about English skills.

Employers report that they are looking for:

» the 'basics' in English;

» significantly enhanced listening and speaking skills;

» good writing, oral and spoken comprehension;

» improved spelling, grammar and vocabulary.

Employers reported problems with some of their potential recruits and young employees who have difficulties in constructing emails, use text speak rather than properly constructed sentences and have poor spelling and communication skills.

When asked, 17 per cent of employers said that maths was their main concern. Employers say they are less concerned about what they consider to be 'academic' maths (algebra, calculus, etc.) but they value practical, applied skills in maths. They identified the kind of skills that they expect potential recruits to have:

» use of approximation;

» mental arithmetic;

» understanding visual data such as graphs and charts;

» a solid grasp of units of measurement;

» the ability to check their own calculations;

» simple problem solving;

» 26 per cent say they are concerned about both English and maths and only 11 per cent say they have no concerns.

This and other surveys carried out by the CBI in 2010 and 2012 indicate the mismatch between skills that employers need and the skills that learners are gaining. The lists above are a useful indication of the kinds of skills that you should be looking to develop in your students. Development of employability and life skills in using English and maths is crucial to the future of your learners. The importance of this is shown by the strong emphasis placed on the development of English and maths skills when post-16 providers are inspected by Ofsted. The following section looks at the revised Common Inspection Framework, in use from 1 September 2015, and highlights how judgements on the overall quality of provision are influenced by the quality of delivery of English and maths skills.

The revised Common Inspection Framework

From 1 September 2015 a revised Common Inspection Framework (CIF) (Ofsted, 2015a) has been used to judge the quality of post-16 provision. The revised framework brings criteria and judgements together in a common inspection framework that can be used across all provisions from nursery to further education.

Inspectors use the CIF and the inspection handbook (Ofsted, 2015b) to make judgements on the quality of provision for all providers. It's important to realise that these two publicly available documents are the only documents on which they base their judgement. There is no secret inspectors' guide or private document that inspectors refer to. You should become familiar with these documents and refer to them when judging your own provision of English and maths.

In their briefings about the revised Common Inspection Framework, Ofsted stated that they want to take the pressure off providers who feel that they have to prepare for inspection, and see 'what you do daily for your learners' (Ofsted Future of Education Inspection launch events: presentation slides, n.d.). This supports the idea that to deliver outstanding development of English and maths skills it is necessary to deliver good and outstanding learning in most sessions. In other words, embedding and developing English and maths skills has to become a habit in all lessons.

Although the main judgement areas (overall effectiveness, teaching, learning and assessment, leadership and management) and outcomes remain, there is a new judgement on personal development, welfare and behaviour. The new judgement clearly involves the development of English and maths skills. Judgements are made on how well learners are prepared for 'the next stage of their education, employment, self-employment or training' (Ofsted, 2015a). The development of English and maths skills is an important part of the preparation for their next stage of learning. It is important to note that development of skills in English, maths, ICT and employability skills features heavily in all judgement areas.

Judging the effectiveness of leadership and management

In judging the effectiveness of leadership and management, inspectors evaluate the extent to which

> "leaders, managers and governors successfully plan and manage learning programmes, the curriculum and careers advice so that all ... learners ... are well prepared for the next stage in their education, training or employment."
>
> **Ofsted, 2015a**

The handbook expands on this and explains that inspectors consider

> "the strategic priority that leaders and managers give to the provision of English and mathematics to ensure that learners improve their levels of skills in these subjects compared with their starting points."
>
> **Ofsted, 2015b**

The 'Outstanding' grade descriptor for the effectiveness of leadership and management includes the following:

> "Leaders, managers and governors focus on consistently improving outcomes for all learners. They are uncompromising in their ambition. They have the necessary resources to sustain provision of very high quality, including in English and mathematics."
>
> **Ofsted, 2015b**

'Inadequate' grade descriptors describe provision that

> " *does not equip learners with the skills, knowledge or understanding required to enable them to progress to their next steps* "
>
> **Ofsted, 2015b, p 40**

All of these point clearly to the role that effective leaders have to play in ensuring that learners are equipped with the skills necessary to prepare them for their future.

Quality of teaching, learning and assessment

Judgements on the quality of teaching, learning and assessment include the extent to which,

> " *where relevant, English, mathematics and other skills necessary to function as an economically active member of British society and globally are promoted through teaching and learning* "
>
> **Ofsted, 2015a**

The handbook for inspection elaborates on this and states that judgements will be made on the extent to which

> " *teaching, learning and assessment support learners to develop their skills in English ... and their employability skills* "
>
> **Ofsted, 2015b**

The grade descriptors for a judgement of 'Outstanding' teaching, learning and assessment include,

> " *staff promote ... English, mathematics, ICT and employability skills exceptionally well* "
>
> **Ofsted, 2015b**

while in 'Inadequate' provision

'learners are not developing English, mathematics, ICT or employability skills adequately to equip them for their future progression'

Ofsted, 2015b

Outcomes for learners

In relation to outcomes for learners the grade descriptors for a judgement of 'Outstanding' provision include:

"the proportion of learners completing their courses and achieving meaningful qualifications, including where appropriate, in English and mathematics ... is very high or improving rapidly."

Ofsted, 2015b

'Inadequate' provision is characterised by:

"Learners [who] have not attained the qualifications, knowledge, understanding or skills they need for the next stage of education, training or employment."

Ofsted, 2015b

Next steps

The CIF places great emphasis on ensuring that students are prepared with the English and maths skills that they will need for the next stage of their education or training. The next chapter looks at how students learn and remember concepts in English and maths and how you can help learners to develop these helpful study skills.

References

CBI (2010) *Making It All Add Up: Business Priorities for Numeracy and Maths*. London: CBI. Available at: www.cbi.org.uk/media/935352/2010.08-making-it-all-add-up.pdf (accessed 2 July 2015).

CBI/Pearson (2012) *Learning to Grow: What Employers Need from Education and Skills. Education and Skills Survey 2012*. London: CBI. Available at: www.cbi.org.uk/media/1514978/cbi_Education_and_skills_survey_2012.pdf (accessed 11 August 2015).

Digitale, E (2012) 'Imaging study reveals differences in brain function for children with math anxiety'. Available at: http://med.stanford.edu/news/all-news/2012/03/imaging-study-reveals-differences-in-brain-function-for-children-with-math-anxiety.html (accessed 24 August 2015).

Dweck, C (2006) *Mindset: The New Psychology of Success*. New York: Random House.

Hindle, H (n.d.) www.growthmindsetmaths.com (accessed 2 September 2015).

The Office for Standards in Education, Children's Services and Skills Ofsted (n.d.) Future of Education Inspection launch events: presentation slides. Available at: www.gov.uk/government/publications/future-of-education-inspection-launch-events-presentation-slides (accessed 23 August 2015).

The Office for Standards in Education, Children's Services and Skills (Ofsted) (2015a) *The Common Inspection Framework: Education, Skills and Early Years*. London: Ofsted. Available at: www.gov.uk/government/organisations/ofsted (accessed 14 September 2015).

The Office for Standards in Education, Children's Services and Skills (Ofsted) (2015b) *Further Education and Skills Inspection Handbook*. London: Ofsted. Available at: www.gov.uk/government/organisations/ofsted (accessed 14 September 2015).

Pye Tait Consulting (March 2015) *Making Maths and English Work for All*, research report produced for the Education and Training Foundation. Available at: www.et-foundation.co.uk/makingmathsandenglishwork (accessed 31 July 2015).

Chapter 3 How we learn and remember

"*Tell me, I'll forget. Show me, I'll remember. Involve me, I will learn.*"

Traditional Chinese proverb

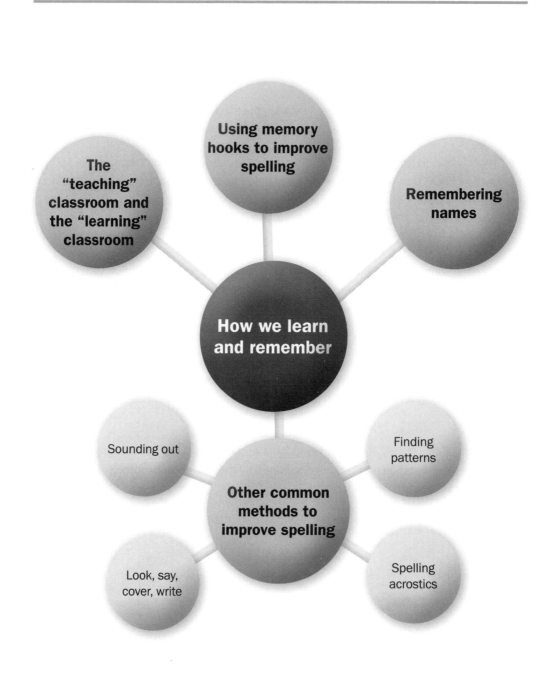

Introduction

This chapter looks at how we learn and remember. It starts with a method of remembering names and links this to how you can encourage your students to remember key concepts in both English and maths. It explores the concept of a 'learning' classroom and a 'teaching' classroom. It looks at the reasons why students have difficulties in remembering concepts and suggests one method that could be used to address this. The chapter focuses on this method of remembering key concepts and gives examples of how this might be used to develop an understanding of maths terms and also improve confidence in spelling. Tutors are encouraged to try this approach and apply it to other key concepts.

Remembering names

We don't forget names. We never hear them in the first place. How often are you introduced to someone and when they say their name you don't really hear, or you haven't paid enough attention to what they said? Are you good at remembering the names of your students? If not, try the following method. I use this in all my training sessions. People are generally surprised and impressed when I correctly name 30 or so people I have just met. It's a process I learnt a long time ago and this is how I explain it.

Practical Task

» Listen to the name. Give it your full attention.

» Ask them to repeat it if you are at all unsure about it.

» Repeat the name within the first five seconds. 'Hello, Rob, nice to meet you' or 'So, Anita, where have you travelled from today?'

» Now comes the most important part. Once you have heard their name, make some powerful mental image that connects their name and their appearance with something you are going to remember. Use all your senses to make powerful connections using images.

This example will help to make this method clearer.

> ## Example
>
> *In one training session I was introduced to Steven. I used the method above, making sure that I had heard his name correctly and repeated it within the first five seconds. He was a tall, slightly balding man with broad shoulders. I was reminded of the Olympic rower, Sir Steven Redgrave. I put the method into practice and made a powerful mental image of Steven in front of me. I saw him in his Olympic vest, with five gold medals around his neck, oars across his chest. I could see him clearly, feel the wind off the water and hear the knocking of the boat against the bank.*

This may seem excessive but the more powerful the image the more memorable it will be. Once this image is fixed – and with 30 years of practice I can do this in a few seconds – I make no effort to remember it. I move on to the next person and repeat the process. At my peak I can remember up to 100 names. I couldn't do this if I tried to hold them all in my head. I rely on the power of the image that I fix in the few seconds I am talking to them and trust that when I look at them again, something about their appearance will trigger this memory or 'hook' and I will be able to recall their name. And it works. On the rare occasion it doesn't work it is because I have not put enough effort into creating the mental image. Try it yourself. Start with a few people and follow the system and see if the mental image will come back and help you remember their names.

You can adapt the method above to your teaching and learning by using these 'hooks' to help learners recall information.

The 'teaching' classroom and the 'learning' classroom

Consider a scenario where you are recapping on previous learning. Students are asked to explain the difference between area and perimeter. You ask for explanations and no students answer. You might say something like, 'But we did this last week.' Is this situation familiar? You are recapping information already covered but students don't remember. Why don't they remember? Why are they unable to recall information that was covered recently? To consider this look at the examples below. I have divided them into what I call the 'teaching' classroom and the 'learning' classroom.

The teaching classroom

Example

A student says, 'I always get area and perimeter confused.' You address this and explain. 'Well, area is length times breadth and perimeter is measured all the way round. Do you understand that?' The student says 'Yes.' 'Any questions?' The student says 'No' and you move on to the next topic. Do you think the student has understood? Will they be able to recall that information in the future? Almost certainly not. This is what happens in the 'teaching' classroom.

Now let's have a look at what happens in the 'learning' classroom.

The learning classroom

Example

Let's assume the same scenario. The student is unclear about the difference between area and perimeter. You explain the difference and ask if the student has understood. Again the student says 'Yes', but you are not content to leave it at that. You check the student's understanding, perhaps by asking, 'OK then, can you explain to the group the difference between area and perimeter?' If the student has understood correctly they should be able to do this.

There is then one further, vitally important step. Once a student has understood a concept such as the difference between area and perimeter, encourage them to think of a way to remember this difference. Students might find their own way to remember. For example one student said, 'I remember the perimeter is all the way around because perimeter has got the word "rim" in it and a rim is something all the way around a glass.' Another said 'When I see "perimeter", I think of a perimeter fence around a prison with guard towers and a barbed-wire fence and I remember that perimeter is all the way around.' These are memorable images that students have created for themselves, which are going to help them recall the difference between these terms. In the same way that you can use powerful mental images to recall names, students can use this method to recall information.

Reflective Task

» What do you think are the key differences between the 'teaching' classroom and the 'learning' classroom?

What methods could you use to check learners' understanding?

How can you encourage learners to be creative in thinking of ways to remember key concepts in English and maths, such as the correct use of apostrophes or which is the y axis and which the x axis on a graph? Try to be specific.

How can you move from a 'teaching' approach, which centres on you passing on information, to a 'learning' approach, which encourages learners to understand and remember key concepts in their own unique ways?

Why do learners have difficulty remembering the information in the example of the 'teaching' classroom above? I would suggest it is for two main reasons:

1. they have not sufficiently understood and 'learnt' the concept;

2. they have not been encouraged to remember the key concept in a way that makes sense to them.

Often, tutors will give students ways to remember things. For example, you might suggest that students remember the spelling of 'necessary' with the phrase 'It is necessary, on a shirt, to have one **c**ollar and two **s**leeves' as a way of remembering that necessary is spelt with one 'c' and two 's's'. However, this method is your method, not the students'. It is often more effective to encourage students to find ways to remember that mean something to them, rather than accept ideas given by you.

Using memory hooks to improve spelling

Students very rarely spell whole words incorrectly. Usually there will be some part of the word which causes difficulty. Think of the word 'believe'. Which part do you think causes problems? Almost certainly the combination of 'ie' after the letter 'l'. (You might use the rule of 'i before e except after c', which would work here, but in my experience students find this difficult to apply because of the many exceptions.) Using memory hooks encourages students to look at words, identify the part that they have difficulty with and use the image method to find a 'hook' that will help them remember the correct sequence of letters. Let's use the following spellings to illustrate this. Look at the following words: 'desperate', 'separate', 'friends', 'banana'. These are all words that students have difficulty with but have used this method successfully to improve their spelling.

Examples

1. Sean had difficulties with spelling the words 'desperate' and 'separate'. He was never sure which contained 'pe' and which was spelt with a 'pa'. Sean was helped to identify the correct spelling and then challenged to think of a way to remember this, using the memory hook method. He came up with an inventive (if rather impolite) way to remember! He said, *'Well, if you are desperate, what might you be desperate for?'* His answer reminded him that desperate is spelt with a 'pe' rather than a 'pa'. He never spelt that word incorrectly again. Additionally, knowing that desperate is spelt with a 'pe' helped him to remember that 'separate' is spelt with a 'pa'. The use of this memory hook, and associating the spelling with something he could remember, gave him a sense of certainty about the spelling of these words. He was no longer unsure or guessing the sequence of letters. The memory hook gave him a way to remember, which increased his confidence in his spelling.

2. Anita was always unsure of the spelling of the word 'friends'. She could never remember whether it started 'fri' or 'fre'. She was challenged to find a memory hook that worked for her and came up with the thought that she usually meets her friends on a Friday. She visualised meeting them in a place with a large calendar on the wall, the kind that just has the first three letters of the day of the week. She had created a powerful mental image of being with her friends, enjoying herself and seeing this large calendar with the letters 'Fri' in bold, red letters. This image helped to remove her doubt about the start of the word and she used it every time she had to spell 'friends'.

3. Finally, Laura was a catering student in Liverpool. She could never remember how to spell the word 'banana' and she was embarrassed about looking it up in the dictionary every time she came to write it. She was unsure whether there are two or three 'n's' in the word. Challenged to come up with a memory hook, she devised a simple but highly effective way of remembering. She asked herself, *'How many ends does a banana have?'* Her answer was, *'only two, a top end and a bottom end'.* To her ear, the word 'end' sounded just like 'n' and she had her memory hook. A banana has only two ends, so the word banana has only two 'n's'.

The examples above are just a few illustrations of how this method can be used to encourage learners to find ways to remember spellings. It can also be adapted to find ways to remember any key concepts in learning English and maths.

Next, it is important to understand how these memory aids can be moved from short-term to long-term memory. Try the method outlined below.

Encourage students to keep a learning log, either on paper or electronically. The learning log should include new learning. For example, when a student comes across a new, potentially difficult spelling, ask them to record it in a learning log, such as the example in Appendix 2. The most important part of this log, and how it differs from many other spelling or learning logs, is the final column, where the student should record their memory hook and then revisit it occasionally to reinforce their learning.

Using memory hooks is one approach to improving spelling, but there are others. Try to adopt some of the common methods of improving spelling outlined below.

Other common methods to improve spelling

Sounding out

Ask students to break down difficult words into syllables and sound them out (in their heads). For example, business becomes bus-i-ness. Beautiful is be-a-u-ti-ful. It also works well for words like 'environment' and 'Wednesday'.

Spelling acrostics

In this method letters are used to make a phrase to assist with remembering the correct sequence. For example, to remember the spelling of the word 'necessary' you could remember, 'Never Eat Chips, Eat Salad Sandwiches And Remain Young'. 'Rhythm' can be a difficult word to spell, but not if you remember that rhythm, 'Really Has Your Two Hips Moving'. These are suggested acrostics, and students can use them, but it is more effective if students devise their own. For example, students could be invited to make acrostics to remember the correct spelling of the word 'diarrhoea'!

Finding patterns

Encourage students to find patterns of letters in words. This way the same pattern can help them be confident about spelling these words. Examples include words like 'traffic', 'panic' and 'picnic' –all ending in the same 'ic' pattern. Look back at Chapter 1 (p 14) for an example of how you might include this in your feedback to students.

Look, say, cover, write

This method can be very effective for some learners. It involves four steps:

1. **Look** at the word that you have difficulty with. Really look at it and pay particular attention to the part of the word that gives you difficulty.

2. **Say** the word to yourself, breaking down the syllables if necessary.

3. **Cover** the word with your hand or a piece of paper.

4. **Write** out the word below. Once you have done this reveal the word to see if you were correct.

Learners will often ask for the spelling of a word. If you, or any learning support staff, are in the habit of spelling words out for learners, I strongly recommend that you stop this practice. Spelling words out verbally for students has little effect on improving their spelling and you are encouraging a dependency culture. Next time the learner wants to know a spelling, what will they do? They will ask you again and very little learning or improvement will happen.

If a learner asks you for a spelling, try this:

Practical Task

Say 'Have a go yourself on this piece of paper, it doesn't matter if you get it wrong.' Have a scrap piece of paper to hand so that students can write down the words. Something about the fact that it is a scrap of paper and not their final work, tied in with the phrase 'it doesn't matter if you get it wrong', frees the student to have a go at the spelling. Often they will get it right, in which case you can praise them and ask how they remembered the correct spelling. If their spelling is incorrect, look at the part of the word that they have trouble with and help them with one of the strategies outlined above.

Next steps

In this chapter we have looked at ways to improve learners' retention and recall of key concepts and how these techniques may be used particularly to develop learners' spelling skills. In the next chapter we look at embedding and developing English and maths skills in action. Through the use of a number of real case studies you are invited to consider examples of embedding and reflect on what makes them effective and how they could be improved.

Chapter 4 Case studies in embedding English and maths

Reflective Task

Comments

Case study 1: IT and business (Inadequate)

Case study 2: Customer service (Requires improvement)

Comments

Reflective Task

Case studies in embedding English and maths

Case study 4: Engineering (Outstanding)

Case study 3: Child care (Good)

Reflective Task

Comments

Comments

Reflective Task

A student satisfaction questionnaire asks,

"Do you have any suggestions to improve the course?"

The student writes,

"Nothing enjoyable."

What he meant to say was,

"Nothing. Enjoyable."

The absence of the full stop has changed the meaning entirely. Unfortunately, the tutor did not pick up on this as an opportunity to reinforce the importance of correct punctuation!

Introduction

This chapter looks at four case studies of observed lessons. The judgements made on embedding English and maths in the lessons cover all four possible Ofsted grades (Grade 1, Outstanding; Grade 2, Good; Grade 3, Requires Improvement; and Grade 4, Inadequate) and were agreed with the management of the colleges concerned and a practising inspector.

For each case study there is a brief description of what happened in the lesson, followed by a commentary on the key points. Each case study has a reflective task inviting you to consider what was good and what could be improved in the lesson.

Case study 1

IT and business: 'Inadequate'

There were four students present at the start time of the lesson and 15 students on the register. Over the next few minutes other students arrived, bringing the total present to eight students. Students arriving late were not challenged. The lesson started nine minutes late. The tutor told the class there would be a test on their knowledge of parts of a computer. He added that the focus would be on spelling. The tutor said, 'I am not interested in the right answer, just that you spell it correctly.' After the test the tutor made no mention of spelling. Students' work contained errors such as 'unecessay' and 'maintainance'. These were not corrected or referred to. One question on the test contained a grammatical error and asked, 'What is a file manager is used for?' This was not pointed out to students.

The lesson plan included a space to plan how English and maths skills were to be embedded in the lesson. The box for development of literacy stated, 'encourage correct grammar, punctuation and dictation'. There was also a box for the tutor to evaluate every lesson. This box was completed with the same statement for every lesson, 'Good progress, all outcomes met.'

The tutor provided good feedback on the ICT content of the work completed. Written work showed that some students did not have a basic understanding of sentence structure and presentations contained many errors of spelling including 'peformance'. These were not pointed out. Examples of the tutor's feedback on written work included, 'Some of what you right [sic] is muddled.'

Five students were asked why they thought they were developing English and maths skills. One said 'You have to do English and maths. I think it's the law.'

Students were invited out to the board to demonstrate how they had answered some maths problems. Students wrote the answers on the board without explaining what they were doing. Some were not confident to explain processes that had been covered.

Most classroom walls were blank and uninspiring. The room was uncomfortably hot, with the cooling system not working. The tutor said this had been a long-standing problem. There was no recap of learning. Students started to pack up and leave while the tutor was talking.

Commentary on case study 1

» There is an issue with low attendance and poor punctuality. Only half of the students on the register are in attendance and most of these are late.

» The tutor has stated the importance of developing English skills such as spelling, but has not followed this through with any strategies to help students develop.

» The lesson planning and documentation states that 'correct grammar and punctuation will be encouraged', but this is not evident in practice. It is not clear what 'dictation' means in this context.

» Errors of spelling and grammar in the students' (and tutor's) work are not corrected.

» Students' comments, such as 'it's the law', indicate that they do not see the relevance or importance of developing English, maths or employability skills.

» There are missed opportunities to develop literacy and particularly oracy skills. For example, students could explain what they are doing when they come to the front to answer maths problems.

Reflective Task

» This session was judged to be Grade 4, Inadequate. Do you agree with this judgement?

» What do you think are the key factors that led to the judgement of Inadequate?

» What can the tutor do about the low attendance in the lesson?

» How could the tutor have made better use of the first nine minutes of the lesson?

» Look at the comments in the lesson planning document. How could these be made more effective?

» How could the tutor improve the effectiveness of feedback on students' written work?

» Can the tutor do anything about the classroom environment? For example, the blank walls and the heating problem?

Case study 2

Customer service: 'Requires improvement'

The lesson was a customer service class with ten learners. One learning support assistant was present to support a wheelchair-using student and a student with dyslexia. The tutor started by asking the whole class, 'What is the most important thing in providing good customer service?' Some students made suggestions, one or two were talking while the tutor was talking and one student was checking his email. One student suggested, 'polite, good manners', another suggested, 'communication'. A third student suggested, 'eye contact and facial expressions'. The tutor wrote the ideas on the whiteboard. Although a few students were making suggestions, others did not show a good understanding of the work covered and not all students were listening while the tutor was giving instructions. One student used mildly inappropriate language, which went unchallenged. Students were given sheets with customer-service problems on them. They were asked to work in small groups to prepare a role play of the scenario. The tutor was working hard to provide one-to-one support for students by going around the room, questioning students and checking understanding of the task. There was some good one-to-one coaching from the support assistant, who was assigned to two students but supported the tutor by helping other learners as well. Some good learning was taking place in pairs and small groups where students took opportunities to learn from each other. Students' writing contained spelling errors such as 'pirority' for 'priority' and 'keybored' for 'keyboard'. These had not been picked up and corrected. The tutor gave instructions for carrying out the role play, but was interrupted by a student who asked for a pen. The tutor stopped giving instructions to find a pen for the student. The class was asked to listen while each group carried out the role play. While some learners paid attention to the role play group, others ignored them.

Commentary on case study 2

» There is some development of English skills in the class, particularly when learners are working in small groups and when they are supported one to one by the tutor or learning assistant. There are no naturally occurring opportunities to develop maths skills.

» There are missed opportunities to develop the spelling of vocationally relevant words such as 'priority' and 'keyboard'.

» The planned learning does not fully meet the needs of learners. This is a lively group that would have benefited from a more structured approach to the topic. For example, carrying out role plays while the rest of the class are asked to listen is not appropriate for this group.

» There is a lack of clear strategies to deal with low-level disruption from a few learners. For example, learners talking while the tutor gives instructions; learners using mildly inappropriate language; and the tutor stopping instructions to find a pen for one learner.

Reflective Task

» This session was judged to be Grade 3, Requires Improvement. Do you agree?

» What would have made this session 'Good'?

» Could this session be judged inadequate?

» What strategies could the tutor use to deal with the low-level disruption?

» What could the tutor have done differently in dealing with the interruption by the student asking for a pen?

Case study 3

Child care: 'Good'

The lesson was a child-care class with 17 students on the register. Fifteen students were present at the start of the lesson. As students entered the class, a series of random letters were written on the board with students asked to make as many words as possible from the letters. Students were awarded one mark per word and five marks for a vocationally relevant word, but only if the student was able to define it correctly. One student asked, 'Why do we have to do maths and English?' The tutor responded by referring the question to the rest of the class. After some hesitation, students came up with some suggestions such as, 'Because it is important for your future' and, 'It helps you with your career.'

The tutor explained that students would be improving their speaking and listening skills by discussing examples of bad customer service. The tutor gave students some examples of bad customer service from nurseries. The majority of students engaged in lively discussions of the examples.

Most students were fully engaged and often asked questions. The tutor usually started her response to students' questions by saying, 'You tell me what you think the answer is ...' In whole-class discussions students were encouraged to come up to the board to explain answers. At one point the tutor said, 'I would love there to be five people who feel comfortable to come up and explain how it is done.'

One student arrived 20 minutes late to the lesson, which lasted an hour. The tutor stressed the importance of punctuality and asked the student to calculate his lateness as a percentage of the lesson.

Another student asked, 'Does "litre" have an "i" in it?' The tutor spelt out the word 'litre' and said, 'You will remember it now, won't you?' There was a brief recap of the learning and half of the students contributed answers.

Commentary on case study 3

» Students are engaged as soon as they walk into the lesson with the challenge to create words from the letters on the board. The competitive element motivated learners.

» Opening up the question of 'Why do we have to do English and maths?' to the rest of the class leads to some good reinforcement of learning and is more effective than only the tutor answering.

» The lateness is handled well, without too much disruption to the lesson but stressing the importance of punctuality. Calculating percentage of the lesson missed is a good idea.

» The tutor could have asked students for their own experiences of bad customer service as well as providing examples.

» Spelling out the word 'litre' is not so effective. It would have been better to ask the student to attempt it first. The student could have been encouraged to find a way to remember the spelling of 'litre' (see suggestions in Chapter 3) rather than being told 'you will remember it now'.

» The recap of the lesson is a little rushed, with only half of the class making some contribution.

Reflective Task

This session was judged to be 'Good'. Do you agree?

» What would have made this lesson 'Outstanding'?

» How might the tutor link the opening activity to the rest of the lesson?

» What are the advantages and disadvantages of asking students, 'What do you think the answer is?'

» How could the recap of the lesson be improved?

Case study 4

Engineering: 'Outstanding'

The lesson was an engineering class with 12 of the 13 students present at the start of the lesson. Students were asked to design a health and safety leaflet. The outcomes for the lesson were displayed on the whiteboard and discussion of these placed clear emphasis on the importance of correct layout of the leaflet and accurate use of spelling and punctuation. Learners demonstrated through their discussion that they were clearly aware of the importance of these skills. One student came to the front of the class to explain the meaning of the word 'persuade' in the assignment.

Students were encouraged to self-assess and proofread. Coloured pens were available for students to mark their own work. All students worked well and were fully engaged and challenged for the whole lesson. Students showed a keen interest in their work and frequently asked questions to clarify their learning. There was excellent learning taking place between groups of students as they discussed the most effective approaches to designing the leaflet. A classroom assistant circulated and helped students, making excellent use of coaching approaches to draw answers out of students. The tutor agreed a timescale for the students to complete work during the lesson and reminded students of this timescale. If the deadline was not met, the tutor discussed the reasons for this and how delays might be avoided.

The tutor asked searching questions to extend learners' thinking, for example, 'What do you think is the purpose of the leaflet?' Most students contributed and made very good suggestions.

There was an excellent, detailed recap to cover the main points of the session. The tutor allowed plenty of time to go over what had been learnt, including asking for feedback on the good and bad points of the lesson. Students showed that they understood the purpose of the lesson and commented that the lesson 'Gets your brain going'; 'Improves your punctuation skills'; and 'Improves your persuading techniques'.

Commentary on case study 4

» There is a very purposeful atmosphere in this lesson.

» Students are fully engaged throughout the lesson.

» They are clear about what they are doing and what skills are being developed.

» Students ask more questions than the tutor does.

» Both tutor and classroom assistant work hard to encourage learners to think for themselves.

» Students are very clear about the importance of developing English, maths and employability skills. For example, in discussing deadlines, students develop skills such as time management and negotiation.

» The majority of students make very good progress in the lesson.

Reflective Task

» Do you agree that this lesson demonstrates outstanding learning?

» What do you think are the key features of the lesson that led to a judgement of 'Outstanding'?

» What features of this lesson could you adopt in your own teaching and learning?

Next steps

The second part of this book gives practical ideas to help you develop and embed English and maths into your lessons.

PART 2
Practical activities

Introduction to the activities

This chapter outlines 20 practical activities – ten for maths and ten for English – that can be used with learners to develop their English and maths skills. Each activity is spread over two pages. The left-hand page includes notes for you, the tutor. The right-hand page is for use with your learners. All of these activities have been used successfully to develop skills in English and maths. They can be used as they are or adapted to suit the needs and contexts of different learners. The activities are divided into maths and English but each can be used more naturally to develop skills in both areas. For example, in discussing solutions to maths problems, learners are practising speaking and listening skills. Similarly, learners need to be skilled in reading and interpreting information in order to understand what is being asked of them in maths problems. For each activity the tutor's notes are divided into a number of clear sections, detailed below.

How to use this idea

This section suggests ways in which you might use the idea, as an individual, pair or group exercise, perhaps as a starter activity or to reinforce certain skills. It discusses the reasons for using the activity and some key principles that support the learning.

Understanding the activity

This section explains how to carry out the activity together with some ideas about the key themes.

Skills practice

This section highlights the specific skills that are developed in the exercise. You should make your learners aware of these.

Developing employability skills

Where relevant, this section suggests some of the employability skills that are developed through the activity. These are skills that learners need in future study or employment and might include, for example, team working, speaking and listening, and presenting a logical and coherent argument.

Extension activities

Where relevant, some ways in which the activity may be extended are suggested. These are only suggestions and you may be able to devise your own ways of extending the learning.

Answers

Where necessary, answers are provided. In some cases these appear in the tutor's notes, and in other cases they can be found in the 'Answers' section at the back of the book.

Key points to remember in using these activities

» *Try not to use these activities in isolation. Where possible, link them to key learning in the lesson and ensure that learners do not see these activities as 'separate' from the lesson.*

» *Adapt the learning activities to suit the needs of your learners. Use them as a basis to help learners develop skills but tailor them to the needs of your learners.*

» *Ensure that learners understand why they are doing these activities and how the activity will help them practise or develop important skills.*

» *Use these types of activity little and often. Developing English and maths skills has to become a habit in the learning process.*

Taking it further

The following are suggested websites which provide further resources to support the development of English and maths skills.

http://toolkits.excellencegateway.org.uk/functional-skills-starter-kit/section-3-developing-effective-practice/section-3a-resources-support-effective-practice/teaching-and-learning-resources-english-mathematics-and-ict

www.aelp.org.uk/news/general/details/new-english-and-maths-resources

www.bbc.co.uk/skillswise/English

www.bbc.co.uk/skillswise/maths

www.growthmindsetmaths.com

www.mathseverywhere.org

www.nationalnumeracy.org.uk/national-numeracy-challenge

www.skillsworkshop.org/useful_links

Notes for Activity 1: Age and house number

How to use this idea

This is one of a number of activities that engage learners with numbers. It can be used as a short, focused activity to start or end the lesson, or as an energiser. It's important that it is not seen as an isolated activity. It demonstrates that if you can engage with numbers, something that at first appears confusing and mystifying is actually quite simple. Use it to encourage learners not to give up when they see an apparently confusing problem, for example on a test paper. It reinforces the idea that you can have fun with numbers and demonstrates that fear of numbers and the sense of 'magic' about them is used in many forms of selling, often to convince consumers that they are getting a better deal than they actually are.

Understanding the activity

It appears complex but is actually very simple – like a lot of maths.

If you carry out the steps in the following order you can see that it is a trick to get you to give your age and house number and then carry out a number of calculations that bring you back to zero.

Let's look at Terry, someone who lives at number 11 and is 60 years old. Carry out the steps in the following order.

» Step 1
Write down the house number: 11

» Step 2
Double it: 22

» Step 4
Multiply by 50: 22 × 50 = 1100

» Step 5
Add Terry's age: 1100 + 60 = 1160 (the answer!)

The first two digits are Terry's house number; the second two are his age.

Point out to learners that they could have arrived at the same answer by multiplying their house number by 100 because this is the same as doubling the house number and multiplying it by 50. This would make the calculation easier but less impressive as a trick!

The following steps add up numbers and subtract them to get back to zero. In other words, a waste of time, but designed to make the trick more complicated.

» Step 3
Add the number of days in a week: 7

» Step 4
Multiply by 50: 7 × 50 = 350

» Step 7
Add 15: 350 + 15 = 365

» Step 6
Subtract the number of days in a year (not a leap year): 365 − 365 = 0

Skills practice

This is an opportunity to practise the following skills:

» using mathematical operations including addition, subtraction and multiplication;

» following sequential instructions;

» reading carefully;

» using a calculator.

Extension activities

Ask learners to find their own number tricks. They must present them and be able to explain how they work.

Activity 1: Age and house number

Try this: you will probably need a calculator!

1. Write down your house number.

2. Double it.

3. Add the number of days in a week.

4. Multiply by 50.

5. Add your age.

6. Subtract the number of days in a year (not a leap year).

7. Add 15.

The answer is your house number and your age!

Can you explain why this works?

Notes for Activity 2: It's all about attitude!

How to use this idea

This is a good starter activity to emphasise to students the importance of the correct attitude in their learning. It can be done individually or in pairs. You can differentiate by asking some learners to add the figures without using a calculator.

Understanding the activity

Display the grid on the whiteboard or print it out for students to use individually.

Explain to students how the grid works. In this case, the letter A is worth 1 point; the letter B is worth 2 points; C is worth 3 points and so on.

Using the grid ask students to add up the value of the word 'attitude'. Give them the option of adding it up mentally or using a calculator. They should arrive at the answer below:

A = 1%	T = 20%	T = 20%	I = 9%
T = 20%	U = 21%	D = 4%	E = 5%.

The total is 100 per cent!

Now use the same method to calculate the value of the words 'hard work'. This time the answer is 98 per cent. Bring out the point that hard work will achieve 98 per cent of what they want but the correct attitude is worth 100 per cent.

Skills practice

This is an opportunity to practise the following skills:

» emphasising the importance of attitude in learning;

» understanding percentages;

» following instructions;

» reading carefully and learning from errors. For example, if students add up the letters incorrectly, explore why this happened;

» practising and improving confidence in mental arithmetic or using a calculator.

Developing employability skills

This provides an opportunity to discuss the importance of attitude in future work or further studies.

Extension activities

Ask learners to think of their own words and add up the value. Examples could include luck (47 per cent), knowledge (96 per cent), success (89 per cent) and even money (72 per cent).

Activity 2: It's all about attitude!

Letter values			
A = 1%	H = 8%	O = 15%	V = 22%
B = 2%	I = 9%	P = 16%	W = 23%
C = 3%	J = 10%	Q = 17%	X = 24%
D = 4%	K = 11%	R = 18%	Y = 25%
E = 5%	L = 12%	S = 19%	Z =26%
F = 6%	M = 13%	T = 20%	
G = 7%	N = 14%	U = 21%	

Look at the table above. If you add up the value of each letter, what percentage is the word 'attitude' worth?

You can use a calculator or challenge yourself to do it in your head.

Letter	Value	Letter	Value
A		H	
T		A	
T		R	
I		D	
T		W	
U		O	
D		R	
E		K	
Total =		Total =	

Now add up the value of the phrase 'hard work'.

Notes for Activity 3: Cups and coins

How to use this idea

This is a good problem-solving activity which helps you get a better understanding of which learners are confident in solving number problems and who requires more help. Watch carefully as groups tackle this problem. Which students jump in and start solving it, which students sit back and make little contribution to the activity?

Understanding the activity

Students are presented with a problem involving cups and coins. Explain that you are going to set them a group challenge. Ensure each group is no larger than six. Be quite precise about explaining the task. You are looking to give students the minimum information and encourage them as a group to discuss possible solutions. Try not to answer students' questions after the initial briefing. Encourage them to talk within the group to see if they can come to an understanding. The key information to give to students is:

» You have 15 coins and four cups.

» Your challenge is to place the coins in the cups so that you can make every value from 1 to 15 (1, 2, 3, 4, etc.).

» Display the example diagram and explain that if you choose to put two coins in the first cup and three coins in the second cup, you have the values two and three but you also have the value five, because you are allowed to add the cups and coins together. But you can only add. You cannot multiply, subtract or divide.

» The diagram is an example. It is not the correct solution. A blank version of the diagram is available to download.

» You must use all the coins and you must use all the cups.

Answer

The solution is: one coin in cup A; two in cup B; four in cup C; and eight in cup D.

Skills practice

This is an opportunity to practise the following skills:

» addition and recognising number patterns;

» speaking and listening;

» following sequential instructions.

Developing employability skills

This is an opportunity for development of problem-solving and team-working skills. There is also an opportunity to recognise the importance of persisting with a problem and talking about it as a group.

Extension activities

Following the activity, ask students who felt comfortable to lead on this task and who was happier to sit back and observe. Extend the number of cups and coins or find a similar problem and ask the quieter members of the group to take the role of project leader in solving this new problem.

Activity 3: Cups and coins

Work together as a group on the following challenge.

» You have 15 coins and four cups.

» Your challenge is to place the cups in the coins so that you can make every value from 1 to 15 (ie, 1, 2, 3, 4, etc.).

» For example, if you choose to put two coins in cup A and three coins in cup B, you have the values two and three, but you also have the value five, because you are allowed to add the cups and coins together.

» However, you can only add. You cannot multiply, subtract or divide.

» The diagram below is an example. It is not the correct solution.

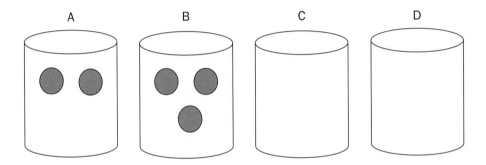

Your notes

Notes for Activity 4: Tell a story about a chart

How to use this idea

This is a good way to introduce the idea of a graph or chart as a means of communicating information. You could use this in any topic area which involves an understanding of graphs and charts. This is an individual activity.

Understanding the activity

Print out a copy of the chart for each student. Explain that you are going to ask them to tell a story using this chart. They can complete the chart with any information they wish. It is a good idea to complete one yourself as an example. If you make your example quite light-hearted it will encourage them to do the same. Ask them to fill in the chart completely with everything **except the title**. Have coloured pens or pencils available and encourage learners to use them.

When they have completed the chart, they should swap with another person and see if each of them can understand what the other's chart is showing. Encourage them to ask questions about the charts. Why is there a dip/reduction between columns 1 and 3 and what could this mean? What is the overall trend of the chart? They can swap with as many people as time allows. You can encourage them to get out of their seats and go around the room swapping charts.

Skills practice

This is an opportunity to practise the following skills:

» understanding the purpose of graphs and charts;

» understanding the importance of a good title (how difficult was it to understand the graph without a title?);

» understanding terms used in graphs such as scales, legends, x and y axes;

» practising labelling the x axis and the importance of correct scaling on the y axis;

» practising asking questions about a graph;

» interpreting a graph and extracting data.

Developing employability skills

This is an opportunity for students to understand how charts can be used to convey information concisely and the importance of considering your audience when creating any form of communication.

Extension activities

Ask learners to create their own charts and extend this to different types of charts and graphs such as pie charts and line graphs.

Activity 4: Tell a story about a chart

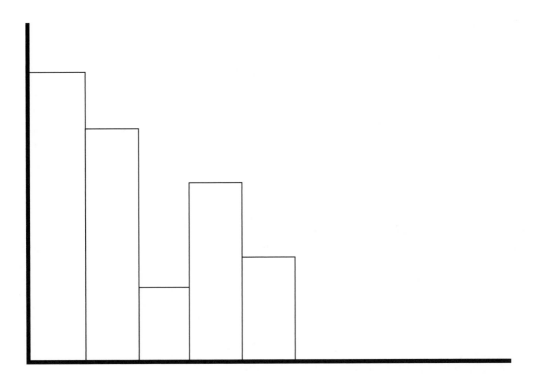

Notes for Activity 5: Mind reading with maths

How to use this idea

This is a paired activity that can be used as a starter or an energiser to break up the lesson. It is designed to help learners overcome a fear of numbers, to engage with them and to be interested in what you can do with numbers.

Understanding the activity

Cut out the activities and put them in separate envelopes. Hand them out, ensuring each member of the pair has a different activity.

Ask learners to guide their partner through the activity using the instructions on the card. Once completed, ask learners to discuss how they think these tricks work.

Activity A: Finding your birthday: how it works

Use D as the day number and M as the month number. After the seven steps the expression for their calculation is: $5 (4 (5 D + 6) + 9) + M = 100 D + M + 165$. You may wish to simplify this for students by explaining that the calculations give the day, times 100, plus the month, plus 165. If you subtract the 165, what will remain will be the day in hundreds plus the month.

Activity B: Guess the numbers: how it works

Any sequence of numbers between 1 and 20, totalled and divided by 3, will give the middle number of the sequence. For example, if the numbers chosen are 4, 5 and 6, these numbers totalled equal 15. Fifteen divided by 3 equals 5, which is the middle number of the sequence 4, 5 and 6. You could invite students to find the highest numbers which still work.

Skills practice

This is an opportunity to practise the following skills:

» using mental arithmetic;
» following sequential instructions;
» reading carefully;
» using a calculator.

Developing employability skills

This is an opportunity for development of problem-solving skills and working with a colleague as learners are challenged to think about why this works.

Extension activities

Ask learners to find their own number tricks. They must present them and be able to explain how they work.

Activity 5: Mind reading with maths

A: Finding your birthday

Tell your partner you are going to guess their birthday. Ask your partner to follow the instructions below using a calculator. Make sure they press the equals key after each step.

1. Enter the number of their birthday. For example if they were born on 15 June, they would enter the number 15.

2. Multiply that by 5.

3. Add 6.

4. Multiply that total by 4.

5. Add 9.

6. Multiply this total by 5.

7. Ask them to add to that total the number of the month in which they were born. If they were born in January add 1, February add 2, and so on up to December, when they would add 12.

8a. Ask them for the total and in your head or on a piece of paper, subtract 165. The total is the day and month of their birthday. For example, 1411 would mean they were born on 14 November.

Or

8b. Take the calculator from them and subtract 165 from the total. Show them the answer, which is the day and month of their birthday, for example anyone born on 15 June will show the numbers 1506!

B: Guess the numbers

Tell your partner you are going to read their mind!

1. Ask your partner to think of three consecutive numbers between 0 and 20. For example, 1, 2, 3; 7, 8, 9; or 18, 19, 20.

2. Ask them not to tell you what they are, but just to think of them.

3. Ask your partner to add up the numbers they have thought of. For example 1, 2, 3 would total 6; 7, 8, 9 would total 24; and 18, 19 and 20 would total 57.

4. They should tell you the total of the numbers.

In your head or on a piece of paper divide this total by 3. The answer will be the middle number of their three numbers. For example, if they chose 1, 2 and 3, the total will be 6. Divide 6 by 3 and the answer is 2. This is the middle number of their sequence 1, 2, 3.

Notes for Activity 6: Bedroom makeover

How to use this idea

This is a useful individual or paired activity. For learners, facing 10 or 20 questions on a test paper can be daunting. This activity breaks down each question into an individual task. Look at the two example questions. These could be cut out and laminated to make individual tasks. Devise some of your own or find example maths functional skills questions on most awarding organisation websites.

Understanding the activity

Ask learners to:

» choose one of the questions;

» answer the question, making sure that they show their working out;

» think about the maths skills that are needed to answer this question, discussing these with a partner and making a note of them;

» self-assess which skills they need to develop.

Painting a bedroom: answer	Furnishing a bedroom: answer
Work out area of walls and ceiling $2(2.4 \times 1.8) + 2(1.9 \times 1.8) + (2.4 \times 1.9)$ $= 8.64 + 6.84 + 4.56 = 20.04 \text{m}^2$ Take away area of door and window $1 \times 1.6 + 1 \times 1.5 = 3.1 \text{m}^2$ $20.04 - 3.1 = 16.94 \text{m}^2$ Calculate area painted (3 coats) $3 \times 16.94 = 50.82 \text{m}^2$ Calculate paint (13m^2/litre) $50.82 \div 13 = 3.91$ litres rounded to nearest litre = 4 litres Answer: need to buy 4 litres of paint	Overall cost of items $= £340 + £289 + £85 = £714$ minus 30% (£214.20) = £499.80 Deposit = 15% of 499.80 = £74.97 (leaving £424.83) Monthly payments = £424.83/6 = £70.80 Answer = £70.80 per month

Skills practice

This is an opportunity to practise the following skills:

» mathematical operations including addition, multiplication, division and subtraction;

» reading carefully and following sequential instructions;

» problem solving.

Developing employability skills

This is an opportunity for development of skills working with space and measurement.

Extension activities

Build a bank of these types of questions for learners to practise. You could also ask learners to devise their own questions.

Activity 6: Bedroom makeover

A: Painting a bedroom

You need to decorate and furnish a bedroom. It is the shape of a cuboid.

It has length 2.4m, width 1.9m and height 1.8m.

It has a door width 1m and height 1.6m and a north-facing window width 1.5m and height 1m.

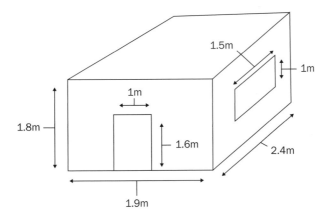

How many litres of paint will you need to buy to give the walls and ceiling three coats of paint, if the coverage is 13m² per litre? (Do not paint the door or window.) Give your answer to the nearest litre.

B: Furnishing a bedroom

You need to furnish a bedroom.

You buy a bed, a wardrobe and a chair in the sale.

The original prices were:

Bed £340.00

Wardrobe £289.00

Chair £85.00

The sale price is 30 per cent off the original price.

The shop offers an interest-free deal of 15 per cent deposit and six regular monthly payments.

Work out the cost of the deposit and each monthly payment. Show all your workings.

Notes for Activity 7: Discrimination legislation questions

How to use this idea

This activity combines knowledge of the history of discrimination legislation with opportunities to practise reading and maths skills. Use it as an individual or group activity to reinforce knowledge of discrimination legislation as well as practising accurate reading.

Understanding the activity

Ask learners to look at the information sheet on the history of discrimination legislation. Use the questions below, or create your own. Ensure learners show their working out.

Question	Working out	Answer
1 How many years ago was the Lunatics Act introduced?		
2 How many years were there between the Lunatics Act and the Idiots Act?		
3 What was introduced 100 years after the Idiots Act?		
4 How many years after the National Assistance Act was the Disabled Persons Act introduced?		
5 How old would someone who is now 25 have been when the Disability Discrimination Act was introduced?		
6 How old would someone now be who was 18 when the Chronically Sick & Disabled Persons Act was introduced?		
7 How old would someone now be who was 20 when the Carers and Disabled Children's Act was introduced?		
8 How old would someone now be if they were born five years before the UN Convention on the Rights of Persons with Disabilities was introduced?		

Skills practice

This is an opportunity to practise the following skills:

» mathematical operations including addition and subtraction;
» reading carefully and carrying out calculations using time;
» considering language used in legislation and how it has changed over the years.

Developing employability skills

Knowledge of legislation is useful in vocational areas like care and social work.

Extension activities

Ask learners to devise their own questions on the information for other learners to answer.

Activity 7: Discrimination legislation questions

1845: The Lunatics Act was an Act to regulate private madhouses.

1886: The Idiots Act provided separately for idiots and imbeciles, which was the Victorian definition of learning disability,

1913: The Mental Deficiency Act provided for the segregation of *'mental defectives'*.

1927: The Mental Deficiency Act updated the 1913 Act and emphasised the need for care outside institutions.

1930: The Mental Treatment Act allowed for voluntary admissions.

1948: The National Assistance Act made provisions in the community, or residential settings for those in need.

1959: The Mental Health Act defined mental disorder, which is mental illness as distinct from learning disability.

Discrimination legislation

1970: The Chronically Sick & Disabled Persons Act was the first in the world to recognise and give rights to people with disabilities.

1986: The Disabled Persons Act required social services to provide a written assessment of disabled people.

1995: The Disability Discrimination Act gives rights to disabled people to prevent discrimination on the grounds of disability.

1998: The Human Rights Act. This legislation adopted the European Convention on Human Rights into British law.

2000: Carers and Disabled Children Act 2000. Young disabled people aged 16 and 17 became eligible to receive direct payments to purchase their own care support.

2007: The Mental Health Act amended and reformed the Mental Health Act 1983. It defines mental disorder as *'any disorder or disability of the mind'*.

2008: The United Nations introduced the **UN Convention on the Rights of Persons with Disabilities,** which obliged members to promote equal rights and root out discrimination.

2012: Health and Social Care Act (2012). This legislation introduced major reforms to the NHS.

Notes for Activity 8: Converting units of measurement

How to use this idea

This is a good activity to introduce the idea of equivalencies and converting units in measurement. The cards contain some easier and some more challenging conversions. You can devise your own cards to suit the level of your learners and relate the measurements to your vocational area or local environment such as distance in kilometres to the nearest large town or the width of a room that learners use.

Understanding the activity

Using the cards provided, or your own examples, cut out the cards and give a card to each member of the class. The task is to find the person who has the equivalent card. For example, if a learner has the card with 8000g on it, they must ask around and find the person with the card saying 8kg. If they have the card with 979cm they must find the person with the card saying 9.79m. Once the equivalents have been found, ask learners to explain to each other why the numbers are equivalent. Additionally they could suggest in what contexts you might find these measurements. For example, 54.61 litres might be the capacity of a car's petrol tank, or 1.3 metres might be the height of a child.

Skills practice

This is an opportunity to practise the following skills:

» understanding conversions between measuring units;

» practising converting a variety of measuring units;

» relating measurements to local or vocational contexts.

Developing employability skills

This is an opportunity to explore measurements used in certain vocational areas.

Extension activities

Learners could be asked to look for examples of three equivalencies, for example centimetres, metres and kilometres, or milligrams, grams and kilograms.

Activity 8: Converting units of measurement

8000 grams	8 kilograms
23.5km	23,000m
80.62m	8062cm
44.51g	44,510mg
54.61 litres	54,610ml
979cm	9.79m
7180mm	718cm
25,400g	25.4kg
700cm	7m
7321m	7.321km
130cm	1.3m
4 litres	4000ml

Notes for Activity 9: Finding faults

How to use this idea

This is a paired activity which looks at recording data, presenting it graphically and making recommendations for improvement. This example uses a scenario of faults in a machine, but it can be adapted for almost any vocational area. For example, it could be used in customer service for the nature of different kinds of complaints; in IT support for the different nature of helpdesk calls; or in child care for the frequency of childhood illnesses.

Understanding the activity

Give each pair of students a copy of the worksheet and one die. Explain that there are six possible faults in a machine that is currently in use. These faults are given number codes as follows: 1 – power tripped; 2 – oil temperature high; 3 – oil filter needs changing; 4 – electrical fault; 5 – output blocked; 6 – no input feed.

Ask one of the pair to roll the die, at least 50 times. The other member of the pair should record in a tally chart which number the die shows and match this to the fault. After 50 throws, the pair swap over and their partner throws the die, while the other records the fault number. The pair now has 100 pieces of data. They should use this data to create a graph or chart and make recommendations on how the efficiency of the machine could be improved.

Skills practice

This is an opportunity to practise the following skills:

» using tally charts to record data;
» deciding how best to represent data in graphical form;
» analysing data;
» problem solving in pairs.

Developing employability skills

This is an opportunity to develop skills in presenting recommendations for improvement based on existing data.

Extension activities

Learners could also be asked to present their recommendations in the form of a written report.

Activity 9: Finding faults

A machine has the following common faults. Roll the die. The number shown on each roll is an instance of that fault. Use a tally chart to record the frequency of each type of fault. Make sure that you have at least 100 rolls of the die.

Code	Description of fault	Frequency
1	Power tripped	
2	Oil temperature high	
3	Oil filter needs changing	
4	Electrical fault	
5	Output blocked	
6	No input feed	

Draw a graph or chart to show the data that you have collected.

What action would you recommend to improve the efficiency of this machine?

Notes for Activity 10: Maths quiz

How to use this idea

This is an activity which uses a quiz to practise and reinforce concepts of percentages and fractions. The questions in the example below are for illustrative purposes. You could use questions which relate to topics that your learners are studying or current news or general knowledge questions.

Understanding the activity

Ask learners to complete the quiz individually. You can use their scores to reinforce concepts about fractions and percentages in the following ways.

Ask learners for their scores. If the quiz is out of five, ask, 'Who scored five out of five?' and write this on the board or flip chart as 'five out of five'. Ask 'Who scored four out of five?' and write it down in the same way. When you ask who scored three out of five, pause and say something like, 'I am getting tired of writing three or four out of five in full each time. Is there a quicker way that we could write three out of five, or four out of five?' If no one answers, write the score in the form of a fraction as $\frac{3}{5}$ and $\frac{4}{5}$. Point out to learners that a fraction is an expression of parts compared to a whole. In this case the 'whole' was the five questions of the test and the 'part' is the number of correct answers. Ask learners for other examples of fractions as parts of a whole, for example one out of two slices is half a pizza.

Ask learners what they would need to do to change their score into a percentage. Explore ways in which learners change fractions to percentages to assess their understanding of this key concept. If learners give you a correct answer, accept this and praise it but ask, 'How did you get that answer?' Constantly asking learners to explain the process and think about 'how' they know something is a highly effective way of helping them master key concepts.

Answers

1. Albert Einstein; 2. Google; 3. Pythagoras' theorem; 4. Archimedes; 5. 'The Reflex'.

Skills practice

This is an opportunity to practise the following skills:

» understanding the concepts of fractions and percentages;

» changing fractions to percentages;

» exploring the process of how students know and understand maths concepts.

Developing employability skills

This is an opportunity to develop and apply the skills of using fractions and percentages in a range of vocational areas.

Extension activities

Ask learners to work with more difficult numbers. For example, what would their percentage score be if the quiz was scored out of eight? They could also find the mean, median and mode of the scores in their group.

Activity 10: Maths quiz

Quiz

1. Who said, '*It's not that I'm so smart, it's just that I stay with problems longer*'?

2. What name for an internet company is a misspelling of a mathematical term for the number 1 with 100 zeros behind it?

3. Whose theorem do builders, carpenters and joiners need to know?

4. Who is said to have jumped out of a bath shouting 'Eureka!' (which roughly means 'I have found it!')?

5. What mathematical term for an angle gave Duran Duran a title for a hit single in the 1980s?

Quiz score [   ] out of 5

Turn your score into a fraction	
Turn your score into a percentage	
What is the mean average score on your table?	
What is the median score on your table?	
What is the mode score on your table?	

Notes for Activity 11: A–Z activity

How to use this idea

This is a team activity which can be adapted for any topic. The example given here is ICT, but you could use it for the A–Z of child care; the A–Z of construction; or the A–Z of GCSE English. It will reinforce the vocabulary of any area and develop an understanding (and correct spelling) of vocationally relevant words. It is useful as a recap of work covered. You may not have time for students to complete the entire alphabet in one session. In this case learners can complete A to M or N to Z over two separate sessions.

Understanding the activity

A maximum of four students per team works best. Ask each team to complete the chart. Learners should think of words connected with ICT beginning with each letter of the alphabet. Explain that learners must be able to give a clear and accurate definition of their chosen word and they must be able to spell it correctly. They will be awarded no points if either of these is incorrect. Give learners time to complete the chart. Around 20 minutes to complete the first column works well.

After 20 minutes ask for answers. If a group has a word that no other group has written they score two points. Any other group can challenge the group to give a definition or challenge the spelling of the word if they think it is incorrect. You, as the tutor, are the judge and your decision is final! If a group has the same word as another group they score no points. Keep a record of the scores. Ensure that the competitive nature of the game does not overtake the learning taking place.

Skills practice

This is an opportunity to practise the following skills:

» understanding the meaning of terms connected with a specific subject;

» reinforcing the correct spelling of vocational/ subject-specific terminology.

Extension activities

Ask learners to give examples of situations in which the words they have chosen would be used.

Activity 11: A–Z activity

A–Z of ICT

Word	Score	Word	Score
A [eg algorithm]		N	
B		O	
C		P	
D		Q	
E		R	
F		S	
G		T	
H		U	
I		V	
J		W	
K		X	
L		Y	
M		Z	

Instructions

In groups complete the chart above. Use words connected with ICT. The first one has been done for you. If you have a word that no other group has written you score two points. If you have the same word as another group you score no points

Note: In order to score points you must be able to spell the word correctly and clearly explain its meaning. If you cannot, you score no points! The team with the most points wins.

Good luck!

Notes for Activity 12: Spelling test

How to use this idea

This activity offers a different approach to conducting spelling tests. It should be used regularly to help learners develop skills and confidence in improving their spelling.

Understanding the activity

Often the thought of a spelling test will create anxiety among learners. It may bring back memories of school, where learners have been embarrassed by achieving low scores or struggled when asked to spell difficult words out loud. This method of conducting spelling tests takes away all anxiety and helps learners develop an individual approach to improving their spelling.

Choose five words for the spelling test. Ideally these should be words that learners are commonly misspelling in their writing. Carry out the spelling test in the following way.

Tell learners that you are going to read out the words in the test. Ask them to listen to the words but *not* to write them down. After listening to the words ask learners to set themselves a target. For example, if they think they will spell all five words correctly they should set themselves a target of five and put this in the box on the sheet.

Read out the five words more slowly now, allowing learners time to write them down. Read the word, use the word in a sentence and then read the word one more time.

Once all the words have been read out and learners have had time to write them down, reveal the correct spellings, either on a flip chart or displayed on the whiteboard. This is important, as it means that learners do not have to spell words out loud. They can look at the words and mark their own work.

Do not ask for scores on the test. Ask learners to note whether they met their target or exceeded it. Point out that learners who did not meet their target have a chance to learn something new.

Encourage learners to use the corrections part of the worksheet and particularly note down how they are going to remember the correct spelling in the future (see Chapter 3 for ideas).

Skills practice

This is an opportunity to practise the following skill:

» improving the spelling of common words.

Extension activities

Learners should progress to increasingly challenging words.

Activity 12: Spelling test

» Listen to the five words.

» Write down how many you think you will spell correctly.

» No one will ask you how many you got right.

1. _

2. _

3. _

4. _

5. _

I think I will get ☐ /5 correct.

I actually scored ☐ /5 correct.

Corrections

My spelling	Corrected spelling	How I will remember it

Notes for Activity 13: Apostrophes

How to use this idea

The correct use of apostrophes is a skill which many learners find difficult. This activity suggests a method of teaching possessive apostrophes which has proved to be very successful. There is also a worksheet to reinforce the learning.

Understanding the activity

Never teach the apostrophe of possession and the apostrophe of contraction (ie 'it's' to mean it is, or 'don't' to mean do not) at the same time. This can confuse learners.

It is important to follow the steps carefully.

Explain to students the idea that an apostrophe of possession shows that an object belongs to somebody or something. Examples include *the dog's dinner* (where there is one dog) or *the dogs' dinner* for more than one dog, *the manager's office* or *the company's policy*.

Ensure students understand that all of the phrases above can be reversed so that 'the dog's dinner' can be expressed as 'the dinner belonging to the dog', the manager's office becomes 'the office belonging to the manager' and 'the company's policy' is 'the policy belonging to the company'.

Give ample time and practice to ensure that all students are confident about turning the phrases around. Don't underestimate the importance of this step in the process. Only when learners are fully confident should they move on to the next step. Once they are confident that they can reverse any phrase with a possessive apostrophe, use the following process to ensure the apostrophe of possession is in the correct position.

To find out where the apostrophe should go, draw a circle around the thing you are talking about. The phrase 'the dog's food' means 'the food belonging to the dog', so in this case the thing we are talking about is the dog and learners would draw a circle around the word 'dog'.

The apostrophe always goes on the outside of the circle; so that it becomes the dog's food. If there is more than one dog then it becomes 'the food belonging to the dogs'. Draw a circle around 'dogs'. The apostrophe always goes on the outside of the circle to make 'the dogs' food' or 'the dogs' food'.

Skills practice

This is an opportunity to practise the following skill:

» understanding the correct use of the possessive apostrophe.

Developing employability skills

Correct use of the possessive apostrophe is important in all formal communication with potential employers and once in employment.

Extension activities

Discuss the correct use of the possessive apostrophe in formal letters. Learners could try to find instances of incorrect use of the possessive apostrophe and explain why they are incorrect.

Activity 13: Apostrophes

In the following examples, put the apostrophe where you think it should go.

» Try circling the thing that is being talked about.

» The apostrophe always goes outside the circle.

The first one is done for you.

1. It was Tony's car.

    This means, the car belonging to <u>Tony,</u> so Tony's car.

2. How is he going to get to his sisters wedding? (He has only one sister.)

3. It is time to go to Suzys house.

4. What is your babys name?

5. What are your babies names?

6. Pam wants to go to Jessicas party.

7. I'm going to the managers office. (There are several managers.)

8. Sahir is Robbies girlfriend.

9. We refer you to the companys policy. (There is only one company.)

10. My cars tyres were damaged.

Notes for Activity 14: Prefix, suffix and root words

How to use this idea

This activity builds learners' spelling skills and vocabulary. As well as correct spelling, learners should also know the meaning of the word and in what context it may be used. They can work individually or in pairs. Use the example table or devise your own to suit the needs of your learners. You can set targets for learners to find a certain number of words.

Understanding the activity

Learners should build up as many words as they can using the prefixes, root words and suffixes provided in the table. You should draw out the spelling rules when adding prefixes and suffixes, particularly where words change their spelling. You may want to add a competitive element by seeing who can make the most words or setting different targets for different groups of learners.

Skills practice

This is an opportunity to practise the following skills:

» understanding how words are built up from root words;

» using common prefixes and suffixes;

» reinforcing rules of spelling when adding prefixes and suffixes.

Extension activities

Learners could learn other rules where the spelling of words changes with the addition of a prefix or suffix.

Activity 14: Prefix, suffix and root words

» A **prefix** is a combination of letters added to the start of a word.

» A **suffix** is a combination of letters added to the end of a word.

» The **root word** is the basic word to which prefixes and suffixes may be added.

Look at each root word in the table below. How many words can you make by combining:

1. a prefix and a root word?

2. a suffix and a root word?

3. a prefix, a root word and a suffix?

Prefix	Root word	Suffix
un	take	
	spelling	
	understand	ing
dis	miss	
	use	
	cover	ed
pre	fortunate	
	calculate	
	interest	ly
mis	view	
	success	
	design	ful
re	tweet	
	pair	

Notes for Activity 15: Speaking and listening scenarios

How to use this idea

This activity builds learners' speaking and listening skills. It is important that learners have opportunities to *develop* speaking and listening rather than just practising it or reinforcing existing faults. It is vital that there is some feedback on their performance and some clear areas to work on in order to improve. These scenarios enable students to build confidence in their speaking and listening, especially in challenging situations. Learners should work in pairs.

Understanding the activity

Give each pair a selection of cards. Explain that they are in a customer-service role and these are scenarios that could happen. Their job is to work with their partner to decide on what they should do and say in each scenario. For more confident learners, you, the tutor, can take on the role of the customer. Encourage learners to work together to decide what to say in each scenario, in particular the actual words and phrases they will use. For example, what is the first thing they will say? Suggest they make a few notes. You can observe and suggest improvements or challenges such as,

'What if the customer responds in this way ...? 'They should practise each scenario several times until they become more confident.

Skills practice

This is an opportunity to practise the following skills:

» reading and understanding;

» developing communication and interpersonal skills, particularly in challenging situations;

» building confidence in dealing with customers.

Developing employability skills

This is an opportunity to develop speaking and listening skills in a number of vocational contexts which involve dealing with customers. Customer-service skills are considered a key skill by employers and are relevant to a whole host of careers.

Extension activities

Learners should think of their own difficult customer-service scenarios and challenge other learners to suggest approaches to deal with them.

Activity 15: Speaking and listening scenarios

Look at each of the scenarios below. For each one discuss with a partner:

» What action would you take?

» What would you say? What words and phrases would you use?

» Make notes and try each scenario out with your partner.

1. A person drops a £20 note when leaving your shop. Before you can tell them a man picks it up and puts it in his pocket.	**2.** A young girl brings a puppy into your café, where dogs are not allowed.	**3.** You work in a clothes shop. A woman tries a dress on and says she likes it and asks you what you think. You think it is totally unsuitable for her.
4. A man asks to try on an expensive suit but he has very bad body odour.	**5.** Someone pushes past customers to the front of the queue saying they are in a hurry and parked on double yellow lines. They ask you to serve them first.	**6.** You notice one of your colleagues in the pizza takeaway not wearing hygiene gloves. They scratch their head and carry on making pizzas without washing their hands.
7. You have just finished styling your customer's hair. They were not paying attention to what you were doing. They now say they hate it and it is not what they asked for.	**8.** You work in a restaurant. A teenage girl in a family group has had too much to drink and is using abusive language. Another customer complains and asks you to tell her to stop.	**9.** One of your colleagues keeps talking about her boyfriend while customers are waiting to be served. One customer complains to you.
10. You see two women stealing perfume. One is distracting your colleague while the other is putting the perfume in her bag.	**11.** A man comes to your counter and starts shouting at you, saying that the goods he bought are faulty. He purchased them from a different department in your store.	**12.** A woman wants a full refund for a dress she bought. She has no receipt and you don't recognise the dress as one your store sells.

Notes for Activity 16: Fact and opinion

How to use this idea

This activity can be used as an introduction to the difference between fact and opinion, which is important in a number of vocational areas. Divide the students into groups with four to six students per group.

Understanding the activity

Write the name of some prominent person on the whiteboard or flip chart. Choose someone that all students will know, eg David Beckham. You could choose a person that features in your area of study, a historical figure or even a fictional character. Ask students to write something they know about this person on a sticky note. Take care over your choice of words. Do not use the word 'facts' or 'opinions'. Tell them to write only one thing per sticky note. They should aim to have three to four notes each. Give out the sheets and ask the groups to put all their notes together and then for each piece of information decide whether it is a fact or an opinion. If they are unsure they can place it in the 'undecided' column. Students should be asked to justify their choices.

Skills practice

This is an opportunity to practise the following skills:

» understanding the difference between fact and opinion;

» developing speaking and listening skills.

Developing employability skills

The nuances of fact and opinion are relevant to a number of vocational areas, including travel and tourism, and particularly sales and marketing.

Extension activities

Learners could find examples of facts and opinions in a number of different texts including newspapers, holiday brochures and sales material. They could further extend this to highlight examples of fact and opinion in a variety of media, including online material, television and radio.

Activity 16: Fact and opinion

» Look at the name on the flip chart.

» Write something about this person on a sticky note.

» Write only one thing per sticky note.

» Try to write three or four sticky notes in total.

» Arrange your sticky notes under the column headings below.

Fact	Opinion	Undecided

Notes for Activity 17: Answering a customer complaint

How to use this idea

This activity can be used develop skills of reading carefully and responding to customer complaints appropriately. The complaint could be in the form of a letter or email or a posting on the company website. The nature of the complaint can be adapted to suit the context in which your learners are working. Learners can work individually or in pairs.

Understanding the activity

Use the letter below, adapt it or create your own letter of complaint. Learners should pick out the key points of the complaint and decide how they, as members of the company, are going to respond. They should discuss options such as refunds or offers of compensation and plan what they are going to write. They should compose a draft response and pass it on to other learners for comment before writing the final version. Ensure that learners consider the different forms the response might take, for example a letter, an email or posting a reply on the company website or a public one.

Skills practice

This is an opportunity to practise the following skills:

» reading carefully for meaning;

» structuring a response to a customer;

» recognising the appropriateness of different styles of response and different formats;

» negotiating skills and handling difficult situations.

Developing employability skills

This is an opportunity to discuss how organisations respond to feedback and the importance of maintaining good customer relations. In forming their responses, learners should consider how best to balance the needs of the customer against the needs of the organisation.

Extension activities

Learners should discuss how they would deal with the engineer concerned and role play a meeting between the engineer and their manager.

Activity 17: Answering a customer complaint

Mrs Norma Swift
11 Ashurst Road
Lenshire
LS27 9BQ

ABC Repairs
27 High Street
Lenshire
LS14 9AJ
(Insert today's date)

Dear Sir/Madam

I am writing to complain about the poor service I received from your company at my home yesterday. Your engineer was one hour late for the appointment and did not apologise, saying the roads were busy.

Your engineer did not remove muddy shoes upon entering my house, and left a trail of mud in my hallway. I have now had to pay to have the carpet cleaned. Also, they did not have the part that was needed to fix the machine. They have now said I have to wait four weeks for delivery and book another visit to have it fixed!

I am very annoyed that I wasted a morning (and took half a day off work) waiting for your engineer to arrive.

I have been a customer with you for ten years and have never had a problem before. I want to know what you are going to do and how you will prevent the same situation happening in the future.

I look forward to hearing from you.

Yours faithfully

Norma Swift

Mrs Norma Swift

Notes for Activity 18: Creating a leaflet

How to use this idea

This is an activity which involves creating a leaflet and can be used in a number of ways to promote skills such as research, writing descriptive and persuasive language and having an awareness of an audience. Students should work as individuals or in small groups.

Understanding the activity

Collect examples of leaflets and fliers for students to look at. Examples can be found in a number of places such as tourist information centres and charity or health education venues. Explain to students that they are going to create their own leaflet and give them some topics to choose from. Suggest that they choose one of the following or another of their own choice:

» advertise the local area or a local tourist attraction;

» promote health and safety in a chosen industry;

» promote healthy lifestyles such as stopping smoking or eating healthily;

» sell a product or service;

» promote a charity.

The leaflet can be made from A4 paper, folded into three, to create six panes, front and back. Students should decide what information will be put in each of these six panes. They should be encouraged to use both text and images. The example leaflets can help with this. Ensure that students carefully consider the purpose and audience for the leaflet. The completed leaflets can be passed around for students to comment on and suggest improvements.

Skills practice

This is an opportunity to practise the following skills:

» writing using descriptive and persuasive language;

» researching, as they find the information for the leaflet;

» designing for specific purposes and audiences.

Developing employability skills

This is an opportunity to develop team working and editorial skills in order to produce a leaflet. Students should consider purpose and audience and develop techniques of persuasive writing.

Extension activities

Learners should find two or more leaflets or brochures and discuss the advantages and disadvantages of both, including discussing their design and purpose and how effective they are in achieving their aim.

Activity 18: Creating a leaflet

You have been asked to create a leaflet to do one of the following:

» advertise the local area or a local tourist attraction;

» promote health and safety in a chosen industry;

» promote healthy lifestyles such as stopping smoking or eating healthily;

» sell a product or service;

» promote a charity.

Alternatively you can decide on a subject of your choice.

Create the leaflet by folding A4 paper in three to create six panes, three on the front and three on the back. It should look like this:

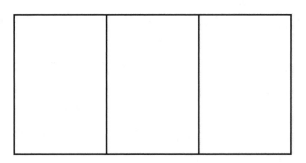

» Research information on your chosen subject.

» Discuss what information you will put in each of the six panes. (Look at the example leaflets from your tutor for help with this.)

» Make sure you use a combination of text and images.

» Ensure that you are aware of the purpose and audience for the leaflet.

» Ask other students to comment on and suggest improvements to your leaflet.

» Prepare your final version.

Notes for Activity 19: Presenting an argument

How to use this idea

This activity can be used to help learners plan and organise arguments for and against a topic. The results can be presented in written form or as a short talk or debate. Learners should work in pairs.

Understanding the activity

The topics for discussion might be:

» Smoking should be made illegal.

» Everyone should be forced, by law, to carry an ID card.

» Capital punishment should be reintroduced.

» Alcohol should be banned.

However, it can be more useful to start with less controversial topics so that learners have a chance to practise the skill of compiling an argument on less emotive issues. Some topics that have proved useful include:

» Parents should not listen to the same music as their children.

» All cars should be painted green.

» All seats should be taken out of public transport.

You could also choose a topic of relevance to your vocational area.

Ask pairs to use the template of the concept map to consider any one of the statements above. Learners should be encouraged to think of arguments for and against the statement. They should also be prompted to think of questions arising from the statement. At this stage they are not expected to have answers. Learners, working in pairs, can have one minute each and choose to present either the case for or against the statement.

Skills practice

This is an opportunity to practise the following skills:

» considering arguments from both sides;

» thinking more deeply around a situation and exploring questions;

» written or oral presentation;

» debating skills.

Developing employability skills

This is an opportunity to develop skills in ordering and presenting a case for or against a statement and to develop confidence in public speaking.

Extension activities

Learners should think of their own statements to give to other students.

Activity 19: Presenting an argument

» Choose a topic.

» Think about the arguments for and against the statement.

» Think about any questions that you might have about the statement. You do not have to have the answer to these questions.

» Use the outline below to arrange your arguments and questions.

» One member of your pair should choose to argue in favour of the statement and one should choose to argue against it.

» You have one minute each to present your case.

» Alternatively you can present your findings in writing.

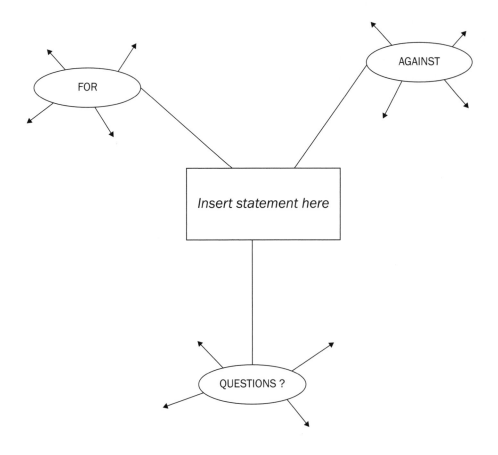

Notes for Activity 20: Providing good customer service

How to use this idea

This idea uses learners' experience of good and bad customer service to develop skills of listening, questioning and summarising in note form. At the same time it helps them to think about how their behaviour can affect the level of service provided and what they can do to improve the quality of the customer experience. It is relevant to most vocational areas. Learners should work in pairs.

Understanding the activity

Ask pairs of learners to look at the information provided on customer service. They should take turns to describe an example of good or bad customer service. As tutor you could also share a good or bad experience. One member of the pair should listen, ask questions and write down, in note form, the key features that made it such a good or bad experience. After one learner has explained an example, swap over and allow the other learner to explain while their partner asks questions and makes notes. Finally, both partners should think of ways that they could improve the customer experience in their setting.

Skills practice

This is an opportunity to practise the following skills:

» speaking, listening and questioning skills;

» summarising in note form.

Developing employability skills

This activity develops understanding of the importance of good customer service.

Activity 20: Providing good customer service

Customer service can make or break a company. In the service industry it should be something that every-one strives to be the best at providing. There is always room for improvement. It is easy to provide good customer service when everything is going well, but really good customer service happens all the time, especially when problems arise and even when you are working in very difficult circumstances.

What is customer service?

To provide excellent customer service you need to:

» ensure that you are treating the customer as an individual;

» be sincere and build a good rapport;

» be professional at all times;

» be knowledgeable about the product or service you are selling;

» get feedback on the quality of service or product you are offering.

Did you know?

Eight out of ten customers won't report bad service. They just won't come back!

Activity

» Work in pairs. Think of a time when you received poor-quality customer service.

» Talk about it with your partner, who should listen, ask questions and make notes.

» Your partner should identify the features that made it such a poor experience, eg being ignored, sales person not listening, etc.

Notes

» Swap over. This time tell your partner about a time when you experienced really good customer service.

» You should listen and ask questions.

» You should identify the features that made it such a great experience, eg helpful and friendly staff, being made to feel special.

» Together list the things that you could do to improve the customer's experience.

Appendix 1
Features of an outstanding learning experience

Chapter 2 looks at the key features of an outstanding learning experience. Carrying out this activity over a number of years has led me to identify the key elements that feature most often:

» Inspirational and engaging tutor.

» Learning is memorable and related to real-life experiences.

» Tutor displays enthusiasm and charisma.

» You accept responsibility for your learning.

» There is mutual respect between tutor and learner.

» Learning is fun!

» There is clear constructive feedback which leads to demonstrable progress.

» The tutor is consistent in their dealings with learners.

» Outstanding learning contains 'light bulb' or 'eureka' moments of learning.

» There is real clarity in what you are learning. Learning is not mysterious.

» You have moments of success and frequent positive reinforcement of the skills being learnt.

» You are motivated to learn more.

» You are allowed to be an independent learner and encouraged to do so.

» You are not afraid to make mistakes and these are seen as valuable learning experiences.

» You see the importance and the relevance of what you are learning.

» Learning is challenging and there is a real sense of achievement.

» Learning is broken down into simple steps that you are allowed plenty of time to assimilate before moving on to the next stage.

» You can see clear progress in your increasing ability to apply the skills you are learning.

» Learning is well structured and you can see how each phase of learning builds on what has gone before.

» Learning has a real impact.

Note: It is interesting that among these key features, subject expertise, ie being an expert in English or maths, does not regularly appear. That is not to say it is not important, but it reinforces the point that tutors, and particularly vocational tutors, do not have to be experts in English and maths to provide excellent support.

Appendix 2 Spelling log

Name:

Group:

Number	Your spelling	Correct spelling	Meaning	How will you remember the correct spelling?
		Write down the words you find hard to spell or that often confuse you. You can get these from your written work.	Write down their meaning.	Remember …

Appendix 3 Assessing writing skills

Use the traffic-light system (red, amber, green) to self-assess your writing. Tick the colour that most applies to you.

» Red: Don't understand/needs work.

» Amber: I think I know this but could use more practice.

» Green: I understand this and can use it confidently.

Skill	Red	Amber	Green	My comments	Tutor comments
Use sentences					
Write in paragraphs					
Proofread and pick up on my own mistakes					
Use capital letters					
Use full stops					
Use commas and apostrophes					
Spell all words correctly					
Use the correct style of writing					
Good conclusion					

What I need to work on in my next piece of writing:

Appendix 4
Self-assessment sheet for maths problems

Tutor's notes

Use the self-assessment sheet provided with learners in answering maths problems.

Describe the problem

Learners should describe the problem in words, for example 'Work out the cost of painting a bedroom which requires three coats of paint' or 'Work out the share of petrol costs on a trip to work'.

Mark allocation

» No error in working shown and correct answer: three marks.

» If they show all correct working and get the correct answer, score three in this column.

» No more than two errors in working and a logical answer (ie correct answer using their figures): two marks.

» If learners make no more than two errors and arrive at an answer which is correct for the figures they use, score two marks. They should correct the two errors in the space provided.

» At least one stage of problem correct, working shown, but incorrect or illogical answer: one mark.

» If learners get at least one stage of the problem correct and arrive at an answer which is incorrect or illogical, score one mark. They should correct the two errors in the space provided.

» Did not show working out: no marks.

» If learners do not show their working they should score no marks.

Self-assessment sheet for maths problems

Describe the problem	No error in working shown and correct answer: 3 marks	No more than two errors in working and logical answer (ie correct answer using your figures): 2 marks	At least one stage of problem correct, working shown but incorrect or illogical answer: 1 mark	Did not show working out: 0 marks	Total /3
		Error 1 Error 2	Error 1 Error 2		
		Error 1 Error 2	Error 1 Error 2		
		Error 1 Error 2	Error 1 Error 2		

Answers

Activity 3: Cups and coins

The solution is: 1, 2, 4, 8.

1 coin in cup A;

2 in cup B;

4 in cup C;

8 in cup D.

Activity 6: Bedroom makeover

Painting a bedroom: 4 litres of paint.

Furnishing a bedroom: £70.80 per month.

Activity 7: Discrimination legislation questions

Note: Answers assume the current year is 2016.

1. 171 years;
2. 41 years;
3. The Disabled Persons Act;
4. 38 years;
5. 4 years old;
6. 64 years old;
7. 36 years old;
8. 13 years old.

Activity 10: Maths quiz

1. Albert Einstein;
2. Google;
3. Pythagoras' theorem;
4. Archimedes;
5. 'The Reflex'.

Activity 13: Apostrophes

1. It was Tony's car.
2. How is he going to get to his sister's wedding?
3. It is time to go to Suzy's house.
4. What is your baby's name?
5. What are your babies' names?
6. Pam wants to go to Jessica's party.
7. I'm going to the managers' office.
8. Sahir is Robbie's girlfriend.
9. We refer you to the company's policy.
10. My car's tyres were damaged.

Activity 14: Prefix, suffix and root words

Some suggested answers
(without changing the spelling):

unfortunately	retake	covering
unfortunate	recover	fortunately
understanding	review	interesting
dismiss	retweet	interested
discover	retweeted	viewing
disinterest	retweeting	viewed
disinterested	repair	successful
preview	repaired	designing
previewing	repairing	designed
previewed	understanding	tweeting
mistake	missing	tweeted
misunderstand	missed	pairing
misuse	useful	paired
misused	covered	

You might also like the following FE books from Critical Publishing

The A–Z Guide to Working in Further Education
Jonathan Gravells and Susan Wallace
978-1-909330-85-6

Becoming an Outstanding Personal Tutor
Andy Stork and Ben Walker
978-1-910391-05-1

A Complete Guide to the Level 4 Certificate in Education and Training Second Edition
Lynn Machin, Duncan Hindmarch, Sandra Murray and Tina Richardson
978-1-910391-09-9

A Complete Guide to the Level 5 Diploma in Education and Training
Lynn Machin, Duncan Hindmarch, Sandra Murray and Tina Richardson
978-1-909682-53-5

Teaching and Supporting Adult Learners
Jackie Scruton and Belinda Ferguson
978-1-909682-13-9

Teaching in Further Education: The Inside Story
Susan Wallace
978-1-909682-73-3

Understanding the Further Education Sector: A Critical Guide to Policies and Practices
Susan Wallace
978-1-909330-21-4

Most of our titles are also available in a range of electronic formats. To order please go to our website www.criticalpublishing.com or contact our distributor, NBN International, 10 Thornbury Road, Plymouth PL6 7PP, telephone 01752 202301 or email orders@nbninternational.com.